Legends
of Mother Mary

*A Biography Based on
Ancient Scripts*

Alyce Bartholomew Soden

Legends of Mother Mary

Library of Congress Catalog Number

ISBN Number 0-9705329-3-8

Fish Rock Publishing Company
33801 So Hwy 1, Gualala, CA 95445-9515
(707) 884-3631 FAX (707) 884-3630
www/fishrockpublishing.com

Copies may be ordered directly from the Publisher for $ 29.95 plus $ 7.95 for postage, handing, and (where applicable) tax.

Manufactured in the United States of America
96 95 94 93 92   10 9 8 7 6 5 4 3 2 1

Acknowledgments

My grateful appreciation to Eva Poole Gilson and Amber Cloverdale Sumrall for their patience, expertise and guidance in proofreading this book.

The New Age Bible Interpretation for permission to use many inspired passages from *New Age Bible Interpretations* vol. IV and VII and *The Life and Mission of the Blessed Virgin* by Corinne Heline. Many thanks.

Special thanks to the staff of Coast Community Library, Point Arena C.A. who sought and found hard to find, out of print reference books.

Many thanks to my dear colleagues of the Coastal Clergy for many years of loving support.

Appreciation for the library provided by my mother, Stella Bartholomew from which most of the reference books came. And to the unseen hand that kept me on task for these many years filling me with ideas and substantiating the material before me.
I dedicate this book to my supportive and loving husband, Jim, managing editor, graphic designer,who completed this project.

i

Preface

The author looked at the materials she had available with the objective eye of a biographer. Having not been raised Catholic and not particularly interested, actually avoiding anything about the Mother Mary until the material became overwhelming, a clearer view of the esoteric level of the mystical happenings became apparent.

It is the result of my curious mind which found very little in traditional scriptures on the Mother Mary. During many years of biblical study I discovered inconsistencies in various writings. The sources range from esoteric, mystical, to transcribed materials from the Akashic Records, scrolls and papyrus.

I present this biographical account to those who are also curious about Mary of Nazareth.

All italics are direct quotes from the source. To the reader not familiar with the language of ancient Christian Mysteries I direct your attention to the Glossary.

Introduction

Some believe that from time to time human beings incarnate onto this planet Earth who are of a higher nature than the ordinary. Some call them "Masters".

It is believed that the Mother Mary was one of these exalted beings and that she was a part of a lineage of at least three generations of Masters. Her mortal life was documented by Josephus in his writings. She was truly a manifestation of the best in human hood.

Mary's earthly mission as the highest Initiate ever to be born clothed in a female body was to prepare herself in body, mind and spirit to birth the Holy Christos and to support him and the resulting church after his death. She also took on the mission of furthering and uplifting the status of women and children in this world. (5.VII. 43)
It is perfectly understandable why Mary's story was omitted from the original New Testament of accepted gospels. The main focus was to be on Jesus, the Christ.

This book is a biographical account of the life of Mary, the mother of Jesus taken from the transcription of the Akashic Records, ancient legends, apocryphal scripts and mystical stories.

This biography reviews the lives of three generations: grandmother Faustina, Mother Anna (Hanna) and Mary, the mother of Jesus. It reveals new information of the life of the Holy Family from birth to death.

Mary's purpose was to birth the blessed Christos who was born a Master and attained the level of the Christ in his life experience. She was an example to the world of the greatest in womanhood.

A Poem to "My Lady"
My Lady is a fragrant rose,
And near to God my Lady grows;
And all my thoughts are murmuring bees,
That haste in silent ecstacies
Upon her beauty to repose.
Sweeter than any flower that blows,
Since all the scents her lips disclose
Are prayers upon the heavenly breeze,
My Lady is.
Her summer never comes and goes
And, for the sweetness she bestows,
My heart's the hive where by degrees
I hoard my golden memories.
For Mary, as my Angel knows,
My Lady is. ----   *Anon. (5IV p.40)*

Table of Contents

Chapter 1

The First Feminine Master Foretold

In the desert country of Palestine was born the highest Master ever to occupy a female body: Mary, the perfected woman, mother-to-be of the Christos.

In Israel before the common era (CE) there lived a group of people whose God-ordained task was to teach Mosaic Law, guide the Hebrew people, and direct the services of the Temple. Among those whose life was dedicated to this office were a group of extremely devout persons, usually very wealthy and exceedingly generous, who often had healing powers, called the Essenes, which means "children of peace." They lived in quiet communities outside of Jerusalem.

According to the Rosicrucian source, many generations prior the family of Jesus were Indo-European by blood residing in ancient Persia and Mesopotania. They were Gentiles by natural religious classification who continued their own mystical philosophical thought colonizing in Israel after the Jews were taken into slavery. The settlement of Essenes in Galilee were also related to those residing in Egypt belonging to the Great White Brother-hood an ancient Gnostic philosophy. (1.1)

The population of Israel was quite diverse as their armies had captured and assimilated many different peoples into their culture. Circumcision and the pledge to believe in the Hebrew God Yahweh and follow the Mosaic Law was the price to live. Many gave up their beliefs choosing life.

The Essenes were a small group living on the banks of the Jordan river or on the shore of Lake Galilee in villages of white washed houses and carefully tended fields, orchards and live stock. Possibly unknown to the general populace, they were often mistaken for Nazarenes. Physically, the Essenes were taller than the average Hebrew with light skin, fair hair with blue eyes. They found ways to formally identify with the religious laws of the land and assimilated quietly with no interference. (1.2)

It was the belief of the Essenes that they would be the chosen of the Lord to birth the Highest Master ever to be born as a woman and through her the Christ. The Messiah was coming as a messenger from God to lead the world into greater peace than ever before. Great souls of this magnitude can only be born upon the earth through pure and holy parents. Mary, the perfected woman and mother to be of the Christos, was born at the large estate of her parents, Anna and

Joachim in Galilee, miles north of Jerusalem.

Her symbol which she carried aloft, was the shaft of gleaming wheat which represents eternal life and the eternality of the divine feminine. This virgin, immaculately conceived, was considered the bride of the Holy Spirit and is symbolized in the Book of Revelation as a woman clothed with the sun and with the moon under her feet.

It was the desire of many Essene couples to birth beings of the highest spiritual level. Many married couples practiced abstinence for long periods of time, performed many physical exercises, such as days of fasting, daily prayer as well as mental discipline from negative thought in preparation for the highest possible soul available being given to their care. Abstaining from sexual practices for long periods of time was common for adherents to this tradition.

Some Essenes were also Levite priests who gave one week each six months to the Temple service of God. The daily duties were decided by lot. During that week they devoted all their time to the responsibilities of the Temple, in prayer, in teaching and in administering the Temple. Their highest duty was that of burning incense before the Lord in front of the golden altar. At certain times of the day,

3

the priest carried the incense pot into the Holy of Holies, knelt in prayer and then returned to report to those praying outside the insights he was given. (1.3)

Immaculate Conception
Miraculous Conception

Generations have confused the terms "miraculous conception" and "immaculate conception." The miraculous conception of the child Jesus was without the assistance of a mortal father. He was conceived by the direct power of God.

"The Holy Spirit will come upon you and the power of the Most High will overshadow you." (1.4)

The seed was planted by the Holy Spirit within Mary's womb, and she carried the child until the seventh month. At the birth she remained a virgin still. Either process is possible as this is a wholly spiritual occurrence.

The Essenes believed that the Holy ones would come through *immaculate conception.* And it was so! Three generations of women were chosen by the Holy Spirit to prepare for the Christos: the grandmother, Faustina; the mother Anna (Hanna); and Mary. Each was

4

immaculately conceived and given to their mothers, still virgins.(1.5)

Immaculate conception refers to the fact that the child's body is completely formed outside the mother's body by spiritual means, as it is said of the Angels. Parents commune on the mental level to conceive the child. The physical body is free from illness, strong and not affected by the limitations of the world. The child is then given to the mother's awaiting arms. This may seem quite impossible to imagine with today's beliefs, but as we ascend in spirituality it will become more commonplace. (1.6)

The parents, greatly advanced spiritually, dedicated themselves to the task of creating these elevated beings. The *immaculate conception* of Mary, Anna and Faustina refers to the pure mental conception by their holy parents as exemplified by the Essene tradition. (1.7)

Chapter 2

Mary's Family Line

Faustina, Mary's grandmother, was born of the house of David to a devout Essene couple. Her grandfather may have been Heli, linking Faustina, Anna and Mary with all the tribes of Israel, in honor and high esteem.

Her family purpose was revealed to her in a dream: "The seventh daughter of my daughter Anna, the wife of Joachim, shall bring forth the blessed moon." Seven refers in the mystical meaning to the Divine Law of Perfection which portends the freedom from the experience of death. This person would not see death, but slip away unaided into the level of Spirit.

Faustina was immaculately conceived and lived her life worshiping and praising God every day of her life.

Anna was immaculately conceived also. Her name means "Virgin of Light." She was proclaimed "more beautiful than the sun and the moon. There were none equal to her in grace, beauty and majesty. (2.1) Joachim and Anna were well aware of the Essene Mysteries and prepared themselves through prayer and commitment to their high calling.

Joachim and Anna choose the purely holy marriage.

Joachim, of the tribe of Juda spent much of his time in the care of his many flocks of sheep, goats and cattle. Though he and Anna had been married for twenty years, there was no child. To be childless in that time was to be without honor, and they were chided for this by their neighbors. They greatly desired a child. Even though Joachim was exceedingly devout as a Levite Priest, his position was often in question for the lack of children.

Many of the Essenes lived on the banks of the Jordan River. They were highly spiritual: dedicated to loving God, loving man and loving virtue. Their highest ideal was to be fit temples of the Holy Ghost. They performed numerous cures of the physical body attending the sick and helpless. Their young were taught humility, purity, and love for all peoples. It was prophesied that through them would come the Messiah. The long awaited Messiah would enter this earthly plain through a blessed Virgin. Mary took vows of virginity and prepared herself from birth for this great honor.

Both Joachim and Anna prepared themselves separately, Joachim in the desert with his flocks and Anna in their spacious home. They prayed and fasted to bring forth the human incarnation of the Illumined One, Mary.(2.2)

Grandmother Faustina's Dream

Faustina considered herself most fortunate with her beautiful daughter Anna and son-in-law Joachim as Anna was highly esteemed in the village among the women. No woman compared to her in grace beauty & majesty. Her marriage to Joachim was pure and holy as they followed the way of the Essenes, peaceful, holy servitors of the Most HIgh. Their greatest desire was to parent a most holy child. It was a sanctified marriage.

As a Levite woman, Faustina had certain responsibilies to assist and council the women of her village. She had accomplished all that she set out to do this day: with providing for the needy family down the way, visiting with Anna, her daughter who was awaiting her expected child, and tending her beautiful garden. There was no urgency in tending her garden; Faustina knew her gardener would gladly do all that was necessary to keep it blooming. She was especially blessed to have all her needs met and with plenty to share, which she did wherever there was a need.

Spending time in her garden was much like the hours spent in meditation: very rewarding. She closed this day, as was her practice, in prayer and thanksgiving to God. The breeze had finally come through the grape arbor giving relief from the heat of the day. She appreciated the coolness as she lay down to sleep.

As Faustina slept, a dream, a vision of light, enfolded her, and the glorious fulfillment of her family purpose was displayed. And she heard:"...Your daughter Anna, the wife of Joachim, shall bring forth the blessed Moon." She saw before her a goddess with azure blue eyes and auburn hair. A great light shone around her. Peace and love exuded from her. While Angels surrounded her, singing praises. Faustina reached out to join in the beautiful song. Then the vision disappeared leaving a scent of the lily of the valley. She awoke rejoicing and gave thanks to God for the great honor being bestowed upon her and upon her children. She now knew her families purpose.(2.3)

Chapter 3

The Marriage of Joachim and Anna

As Essenes, Joachim and Anna lived quietly,
away from Jerusalem about seventy miles
north of Jerusalem on the banks of the
Jordan River. They were exceedingly wealthy.

Many Essene married couples lived together
for years without children. Joachim and
Anna had made a pledge on their wedding
day to abstain from sexual activity until a
soul of the highest caliber would be given
them.

Joachim frequently paid his workers double
earnings and divided his income into three
parts: one for the poor, one for the Temple,
and the third for himself and his family. He
had practiced this since he was fifteen and
he was rewarded with much property and
many flocks of sheep and herds of cattle. He
and Anna devoutly attended every feast of
the year in Jerusalem. (3.1)

One day when Joachim went to the Temple to
give his gifts to the children of Israel on the
Passover Holy Day, Reuben (or Isachar, the
High-Priest) came to him, saying: "Offering
your gifts first is not lawful and will not be
acceptable to God, as you have produced no

seed in Israel. Cursed is anyone who has not
begotten a male in Israel. Go, bring forth a
child, and then come with your offering into
the presence of God."

Joachim was grieved. He went to the record of
the twelve tribes of Israel to find out if any
other Priest of Israel had no children. He
found that all of the righteous of Israel had
fathered children. Even the patriarch
Abraham in his last days God had given him
a son, Isaac. Joachim was troubled and
instead of going home to Anna, he went to a
desert place and fasted forty days and forty
nights, saying to himself: "My prayer shall be
for me meat and drink. Until the Lord my God
visit me I will not go home."(3.2)

Anna had no news of Joachim for five
months. She lamented her childlessness,
and vowed that if she had a child she would
dedicate it to the Temple. Not knowing where
Joachim was and fearing that she had
become a widow, she threw herself on her
bed for a whole day and night. She was so
distraught that she reproached her maid,
Juthine, for not coming to her quickly
enough. When the maid answered her
sharply. She wept even more.

The great day of Celebration (Passover or the
Feast of Sukkoth) was coming, and so

Juthine said, "It's time to stop humbling your soul as the great day of the Lord is here. It's against tradition for thee to mourn. Wear this headband which the mistress of my work gave me. It's unlawful for me to wear as I am a slave: the band has the mark of royalty on it."

Still distraught, though coming to herself she said: " What can I do? I will weep and pray that the Lord my God will be gracious unto me and grant me a child."

Anna removed her mourning clothes, bathed herself, and put on her Golden Wedding Garments. It was about the ninth hour when she went down into the garden to walk. She saw a laurel tree and sat down on the bench underneath it and besought the Lord, crying: "Listen to my prayer. Bless me O God as thou blessed the womb of Sarah and gave her a son, Isaac."

Looking up into the laurel tree she spied a nest of sparrows and lamented all the more, saying: "Woe unto me and my mother who begat me. Even the fowls of the air are fruitful before thee, O Lord." (3.3)

Mary's Immaculate Conception Described

Her beautiful story was given in the apocryphal *Protevangelium of the Gospel of James the Less (Just) not now given in the traditional text. With the coming of the Christ level of understanding to the earth, a new ideal was given. Immaculate conception, procreation can be accomplished by parents whose souls are wedded in a high and holy love, without passion, as a holy sacrifice, the union of mind to mind sanctified by attending Angels. Mary was the result of this form of procreation between Joachim and Anna, her parents.*

Chapter 4

The Annunciation to Anna

Anna spent her days in prayer and meditation wearing her "Golden Wedding Garments," representing her attainment as an Initiate.

The Angel Gabriel appeared announcing the birth of a daughter. "Peace be to thee, O woman. Fear not, for thou hast found favor with the Lord, and behold, thou shalt conceive and bring forth a daughter, and thou shalt call her name Mary; from her shall spring forth the Light of Creation and Him for whom the world awaits. Joachim awaits you at the Golden Gate in Jerusalem."

Anna replied, " I will dedicate her to the Lord my God."

The Angel of Annunciation, also appeared to Joachim in the desert place, saying: "Rise up, O Son of David The Lord hath been gracious unto thy wife Anna. She is waiting for you at the Golden Gate (Jerusalem)."

At the Golden Gate, two messengers came saying to Anna: "Joachim, thy husband cometh with his flocks, for an Angel has appeared unto him."

And she waited for Joachim at the Golden Gate in Jerusalem dressed in her Golden Wedding Garments.

When Anna saw him coming. She ran and threw her arms around his neck saying, "Now I know that the Lord God has greatly blessed me; for behold the widow I thought I was is no longer, and I who thought I was childless, has conceived."

Filled with ecstasy and enfolded in heavenly light as had never been witnesssed, the two Masters came together and multitudes of Angels singing, rejoicing and praising God surrounded them. The Golden Gate is a symbol of two exalted souls meeting on a high level of attainment. (4.1) They rejoiced in the gift they were to receive and dedicated their expected daughter to Temple service.

And Joachim went down and called his herdsman and said, "Bring me here ten female lambs without blemish and without spot: they shall be for the Lord my God. And bring me twelve tender calves and they shall be for the priests and council of elders, and a hundred young he goats for the whole people." (4.2)

As they rested they related to each other

their visions, how they met happened exactly as the Angel had foretold. After giving thanks and praising God, they dedicated their expected child to the Temple, assured that the promise would be fulfilled. (4.3)

The next day as Joachim offered his gifts at the Temple he carefully looked at his face in the priests' shiny fountlet when he went up to the altar of the Lord; and he saw no sin in himself. And Joachim said, "Now I know that the Lord God is gracious to me and has forgiven all my sins." And he came down justified from the Temple of the Lord, he went to his house.(4.4)

Wherever Anna went, the light preceded her. When she visited the sick in the nearby village or encountered a sick, poor or troubled person, they were immediately healed. Sometimes fires fell from her fingertips.The great power of the incoming blessed one, Mary, revealed itself long before her birth.

Joachim and Anna spent their time in prayer and exaltation with only the purest of food, bread, fruit and water. They were conscious of Angelic presences surrounding them and Anna often sang and praised the Lord.

Early in September Anna was informed that

the blessed one was ready to appear. Anna began singing fervent canticles of love and adoration, to the delight of those about her.(4.5) On the birth night as Anna knelt in prayer before her shrine, she was radiant. A super- natural light surrounded her filling the room. She appeared transported into higher levels as Angels sang the triumphant proclamation that the chosen one would be named Mary. As those who were present finally adjusted to the light, they saw Anna clutching a child to her heart. And Mary was born. (4.6)

Anna asked, " *What have I given birth to a boy or a girl? " A girl,*" was the answer. (4.7) Anna exclaimed, " *My soul is magnified this day.*" (4.8) Anna gave the blessed child her breast. It is said that the Angels of heaven and earth saluted Anna for the new life which she would nurture. As the parents watched, the angelic host with vast radiations of light streamed from wing-shaped auras, and they heard the chant of a new day dawning with this Immaculate Conception. They sang: *"The Angels of Heaven and earth salute thee for the new life which you bring forth to the world."* (4.8)

When the thirty days of purification had passed, the baby was named Mary as commanded by the Angel.

Immaculate conception is a prime example of a high initiate demonstrating to all humankind to follow, being freed, forever emancipated from the physical, painful experience of child birth.(4.9)

Chapter 5

The Human Incarnation of The Blessed Mary

Great Joy and gladness came from the neighbors and friends for the loving parents who finally had their dream fulfilled. The Holy Infant Mary was given to her mother's arms early in September. Her father Joachim held a feast in her honor and gave bounteous gifts to the poor, widows and the sick.

Mary entered into human incarnation as a Master Soul. She was in complete possession of all her faculties from the beginning. In other words, she was able to speak and walk about, not helpless as most babies at birth. Her soul expression was love and compassion. Her signature flower was the Lily of the Valley. She was self-obedient, humble, dedicated to selfless service and eager to ameliorate the human suffering and sorrow she found. Her specific purpose was to birth the Christened One. She communed with Angels daily. The Heavenly Host and the Angel Gabriel continued as her guides and teachers on earth, as they had before she came to earth. (5.1)

Grandmother Fastina's dream became reality. Mary fulfilled her life purpose completely. It is said that the Mother Mary did not see death, but slipped over into the level of Spirit looking ageless, like a girl in her teens. (5.2)

It was required of Hebrew mothers that they attend the Feast of Purification at the Temple after thirty days if their child were a girl.

Anna dedicated Mary again to the Temple service and pledged to return in three years to make a full consecration, which would mean leaving her there to serve as a Temple virgin.

Day by day the child waxed strong. When Mary was six months old, to show her divinity, Anna took her to the astrologers (Magi) of the Temple of Helios of which Joachim was a High Priest and stood Mary upon the floor on her own feet facing east to see if she would stand. She walked seven steps indicating her advanced attainment and then returned to her mother. Anna caught her up, saying, *"As the Lord my God liveth, thou shalt walk no more upon this ground until we bring thee into the Temple of the Lord."*

And she made a sanctuary in her bed chamber and suffered nothing common or unclean to pass through it. And she called for the daughters of the Temple that were undefiled to carry her about. (5.3)

On Mary's first birthday Joachim made a
great feast and invited the Temple Priests,
scribes and elders and all the neighbors.
Joachim presented the child to the elders,
and they blessed her saying, *"O God of our
fathers, bless this child and give her a name
eternally renowned among all generations."*
And all the people said, *"So be it, so be it,
Amen."* (5.4) And they brought her to
the Temple Priests, and they blessed her
saying, *"O God of the heavenly heights, look
down upon this child and bless her with a
supreme blessing which cannot be
superseded."*

Then Anna carried her blessed child into the
sanctuary of her bedroom and gave her suck.
And Anna sang this song to the Lord God: *"I
will sing praise to the Lord my God for he has
visited me and taken away from me the
reproach of my enemies and hath given me the
fruit of his righteousness unique yet manifold
before him. Who will proclaim to the sons of the
Hebrews that Anna gives suck?"* (5.5) Finally,
Anna felt freed from the condemnation of the
Hebrew people.

And she laid Mary down on her couch in the
bedroom of her sanctuary, and went out and
served her guests. When the feast was ended,

the priests went away, rejoicing and glorifying the God of Israel.

Anna said to Joachim, *"Build thou a chamber for Mary our daughter that will contain all manner of beautiful things: draperies on the walls and a carpet so that her feet will never touch the earth. A place she will abide until it is time to present her to the Temple."*

So Joachim built for his daughter a beautiful chamber of costly and heavenly things so that she would have her own sanctuary containing an imposing shrine where she found peace and beauty while in company of Angels.(5.6)

From the very beginning, everywhere Mary went a carpet or cloth was spread for her to walk upon. Her feet were not allowed to touch the ground. She was completely sheltered from the world outside their estate

The months passed, and the child grew. When Mary was two Joachim said, *"Let us take her up to the Temple to the Lord, so that we may fulfill the promise which we made lest the Lord send some evil to us and our gift be unacceptable."*
Anna replied ,*"Let us wait."*(5.7)

Journey to the Temple

It was the custom that possible Temple Initiates were examined as to their worthiness prior to their acceptance. To the surprise and delight of the Temple priests who came to examine Mary, they found her wise beyond her years, humble and with a great sweetness of manner. They unanimously acclaimed her a wise and gifted child.

When Mary was three Joachim said, *"Call the undefiled daughters of the Temple, and let each one take a torch and let these be burning in order that the child may not turn back and her heart be tempted away from the Temple of the Lord."* (5.8)

Plans were made to take Mary to the Temple. She had seldom been away from home. Her parents realized that a trip of this magnitude, from Nazareth to Jerusalem could be very frightening as she had seldom been away from the estate. So they planned carefully. They would leave in the evening so that the things of the world would not upset her. They would travel with their wagons during the morning hours, rest in the heat of the day and travel at night. This journey would take seven days instead of the usual four.

Several people would be accompanying them so much food had to be prepared and special clothing for the Temple Ceremony needed to be made. Everyone was busy in the preparation. By sunset of Mary's birthday the wagons were packed. The evening meal was eaten and torches were brought forth to be carried by the seven virgins sent from the Temple. They were a bright and cheerful procession moving along the road singing hymns of praise to God as they journeyed.

In the beginning of the trip most of the people walked. Mary was either carried by one of the virgins or she rode in the wagon. They slept the first night in the open. Up early before the sun they were on their way. Each day followed the same. They saw travelers along the way, and Roman outposts were passed. The way was long and hot, but finally on the seventh morning they arrived at the gates of Jerusalem.(5.9)

A messenger was sent forth to notify the priests at the Temple of their coming. They purchased flowers and decorated the wagons and themselves with wreaths and garlands.

The procession of maidens bearing flowers and singing hymns went first, followed by Anna and Joachim, carrying Mary. It is reported that as Mary entered in at the

Nicanor Gate she heard within her a voice welcoming her, and her body shone with ethereal light.

The Temple at Jerusalem was built on a hill top. In order to enter one had to climb fifteen steps. These steps signified levels of consciousness attained or 'Palms of Degree'. While Mary's family were changing from their traveling clothes to new clean ones, Mary was the first one dressed. (5.10)

Mary was so eager to be set down that she was difficult to hold. Seeing that Priest Zachariah waited at the top of the fifteen steps, Anna set Mary down on the first step. Mary ran up the fifteen steps with ease, never pausing for a moment, indicating her advanced Degree of the Palms.

The priest lifted her up and kissed her and blessed her saying: (5.11) " *The Lord has magnified your name among all generations: because of you the Lord at the end of the days will reveal his redemption to the sons of Israel.*" (5.12)

He placed Mary on the altar, and the Lord God put grace upon her and she danced as if hearing some inner music. Her new dress swinging and her feet lifting. All those present were delighted.

Anne, the holy woman in charge of the neophytes greeted Mary and together with the ten Temple maidens they ushered her into the Women's Court.(5.13)

As Anna and Joachim were leaving the Temple they saw Mary being lifted up into the arms of an Angel and fed from her hand. Mary's teachers were those appointed by the Temple and also the Angel Gabriel.

Anna and Joachim returned home marveling, praising the Lord God because the child had not turned back. They felt confident that she would be cared for wonderfully. (5.14)

Chapter 6

Mary's Temple Service

Mary lived and served at the Temple until she was about twelve. She was taught by the Angels whom she communicated with constantly. The young Mary was often in ecstasy as she communed frequently with the heavenly hosts.

The Temple priests cast lots to see which of them was worthy to become her teacher. Zadok, a man of much wisdom and many years, was chosen. The High Priests blessed Zadok and said to him, "*the Lord hath brought a daughter for you to guide, guard and teach her to go in and out of the Temple of the Lord*". (6.1)

This means, the liberation of the ego from the body in Initiation, "*a process which makes it possible for the individual to visit the Temple not made with hands,*" the inner planes of life and being. (6.2) Mary was educated in the Temple to spin, weave and sew. In addition, she was taught to read and write, which was not a common practice for girls in those days. Her reading lessons were the same as a boy would have had.

She was given a little room overlooking the

Inner Temple containing the Holy of Holies and was assigned the responsibility for its care. Here, her constant praying would not be disturbed. After her Temple entrance she received illumination by the blessed Lord, her son to be, and communed in ecstasy with the bands of Angels singing triumphant songs of love and wonder. (6.3)

"Hail, thou that are highly favored, the Lord is with thee. Blessed art thou among women," (Lk, 1:28 KJ)

The child Mary was addressed by the Angel Gabriel who had attended her as Guide and Teacher from before her earthly birth. She was without fault in doing her daily duties. Her conversations were often started with: Allele or Praise be to God.

The Essenes believed that the Messiah was to come through their followers and many virgins hoped to be the chosen one. Mary did not feel worthy of this honor. Her desire was only to remain a virgin and perhaps serve in the household of the blessed one to come.

Temple Duties

Cleaning the Temple, preparing the incense pots and keeping clean water in bowls for purification purposes was the responsibility of the Temple Initiates. When Mary had completed her daily responsibilities she spent the rest of her time in prayer and communion with her Angel guardians.

Mary's Temple service was a time of probationary discipline preparing her for high initiations yet to come--the highest ever given to one in a feminine body. It required a long and difficult process of sensitization even for one who already possessed great spiritual attainment. Initiation lessons are always the same. The aspirant is lifted to the heights and then tested to the limit. (6.4)

Her daily Temple routine was as follows according to St. Jerome: From 6:00 a.m. to 8:00 a.m. Mary gave herself to prayer. From 9:00 a.m. to 3:00 p.m. she performed her Temple duties and studies. From 3:00 p.m. to 6:00 p.m. she spent in prayer plus many hours during the night. She was constant in her holy vigil, the most astute of all the virgins in understanding God's Law, still remaining most humble in manner.

Mary's loving manner with the younger Temple virgins was noticed and she was never angry with anyone. Every word she uttered was full of grace. She had become a clear voice for God. (6.5)

Years later, during her visit with Elizabeth,
the mother of John the Baptist, Mary
confided to her:
 " *My daughter, you think I had all these graces
without trouble, but it is not so. I assure you
that I received from God no grace, no gift, no
virtue without great labor, continual prayer,
ardent desire, profound devotion, many tears
and much affliction."* (6.6)

Some of the affliction Mary referred to was a
plot to discredit her by the other Temple
virgins. Jealous of Mary's special treatment
and in hopes of having her dismissed, they
made up a story that Mary had in a fit of
anger, hit one of the younger girls. Mary
refused to defend herself against the
accusations and only said words of love and
praise about her Temple sisters. It is said
that her Angel guides covered their faces and
were not available for consultation. She
found herself alone.(5.6) In the end, she was
exonerated. Although she sorrowed greatly,
her prayer was always for those who erred,
not for herself. Never once did the trials she
was facing overcome her.

Her earthly father, Joachim made his
transition from worldly life while Mary was
still serving at the Temple. She was permitted
to see his transition, she blessed him. (6.7)

Anna Becomes a Widow

After Mary left for her Temple service, her parents had another daughter, and they named her Mary also. This other child was given as a consolation, they believed, for giving up their first daughter, Mary.

Anna was still of child-bearing age and a most beautiful, wealthy woman who may have married a man named Cleothis, and they had a daughter. It was important in that day for a woman to be married as she had few rights to property, and it was dangerous for her to live alone. Some financial provision was made to care for the children by their fathers. Mary, being the elder child, probably inherited the greater amount. She was definitely sought after for many reasons.(6.8)

Zavier Describes Young Mary

Zavier's *Persian History of Christ*, describes Mary as *"being of moderate height with a light complexion. Her eyes were very large, almost blue in color, with auburn hair. Her hands were beautiful, and her figure symmetrical in every way. Her personality was pleasing with a sweetness and humility that was noticeable. She remained the same throughout her lifetime. Age did not change her appearance, and in private or public her goodness and dignity still shone.*" (6.9)

Mary Becomes a Woman at Twelve

Mary became a wealthy, most beautiful and sought after woman. Abiathar, the priest, offered Mary many gifts in hopes that she would marry his son. She refused, saying that she had vowed perpetual virginity.(Latin Narrative or Pseudo Melito)

At the time Mary became a woman, the high priest ordered that all virgins of that age who had "public settlements in the Temple" were to return home, and being of a proper maturity, should, according to the custom of their country, endeavor to be married. Other virgins were willing to comply with the order.

Mary was not willing to comply as she and her parents had dedicated her to the service of the Temple. She had vowed to remain a virgin. These vows she was determined to fulfill.

The priest was in a difficult situation; he could not dissolve the vow without disobeying the Scripture, which says, Vow and pay. Nor did he want to change the custom.(6.10)

The Temple Priests, including her teacher Zadok conferred together regarding Mary's future. She was determined to remain a Temple virgin, but that was not possible: as she had reached the age of puberty, and was considered unclean. The Priest said she would pollute the Temple. Mary finally acquiesced on the condition that a heavenly sign would appear to show the way and indicate the person who was to be her husband. (6.11)

The priests recommended prayer to the Lord to ask for counsel on this difficult case. When they were praying, the High Priest dressed in the blue robe of Aaron with the twelve golden bells, went into the Holy of Holies to consult the Lord God. Immediately a voice came from the Ark:

And there shall be a rod out of the stem of Jesse, and a branch shall grow out of his roots. And the Spirit of the Lord shall rest upon him, the Spirit of Wisdom and Understanding, the Spirit of Counsel and Might, the Spirit of Knowledge and of the fear of the Lord . (6.12)

The High Priest ordered that all widowers of the house of David come to the Temple and bring their rods to the altar. A sign was expected that would indicate the chosen one.

Joseph Travels to the Temple in Jerusalem

The aged Joseph was busy at his carpentry work when the messenger came calling him to the Temple meeting. He threw down his adze, took his rod and gathered what else he needed and left immediately as it was at least a three-day journey.

The widowers gathered together before the Women's pavilion and Mary stepped out on the porch. The men gasped. Such beauty, they had never beheld before. They were told that Mary had vowed to serve the Lord God as a virgin for her lifetime, but that was not possible as it would violate the Temple. (6.13)

The high priest took the rods of all present (he thought) and went into the the Temple to pray. When he had finished the prayer he took the rods and went forth, but nothing happened. So he returned again and prayed. Joseph's rod blossomed in his hand and a dove flew out of the Temple and landed upon Joseph's head. And the priest said, *"Joseph, unto thee hath it fallen to take the virgin of the Lord and keep her for thyself."* The crowd sighed. No other man in all Judea was so closely attuned to God. He was considered a saint come to earth by his people.

Instantly, Joseph knew that the great purpose

for which he had been preparing was about to begin. It is said that at the moment his staff changed in his hand and became a stem of blossoms, Joseph's whole earthly life passed before him. Then his purpose became clear. His entire life had been spent in preparation for this great mission.

The white dove's participation in the Mystery sign was said to have been the instrument through which the Holy Ghost acted to bring the Bride of the Holy Ghost, Mary, the virgin to the next act of the holy drama.

And Joseph refused, saying: *"I have sons, and I am an old man, but she is a girl: lest I become a laughing stock to the children of Israel."* The priest said unto Joseph, *"Fear the Lord thy God, and remember what things God did unto Dathan, and Abiron and Kore, how the earth cleave and they were swallowed up because of their gain saying. Now fear thou, Joseph, lest it be so in thine house."* And Joseph was afraid, and took her to care for her. (6.14)

The Priest decreed that the Heavenly sign had been given and Mary became the ward of Joseph which served both their purposes the best. Mary recognized Joseph as her caretaker and her path became clear as told in the Akashic Records. Mary and Joseph were Essenes and had dedicated their lives to the highest initiatory Order. As both Joseph and Mary were Masters, it was a great sacrifice for them to incarnate into the world. (5.14) But being Joseph's ward left Mary free to continue as a virgin as she had vowed. Seven virgins of the Temple accompanied Mary to Joseph's home. .(Latin Narrative or Pseudo-Melito) (6.15)

Joseph considered it an additional responsibility, but he finally agreed to take her into his care and protection as a ward. Mary was no longer referred to as his future wife.

The Master Mary spent many hours in prayer after leaving the Temple. It was this time when she began preparations for the Miraculous Conception and was completely occupied. (5.16)

Joseph was a house builder and left Mary in his home with the seven virgins. He was gone for three years--until Mary was about sixteen.

Chapter 7

Who Was Joseph ?

Joseph of the house of David was an aged man of eighty-nine years when Mary was finishing her time in the Temple. He has been described as very active and able to manage his family of six children, the youngest of whom may have been James, The Just, an Apostle of Jesus and the leader of the first Christian Church in Jerusalem. The ancient legends refer to Joseph as having great wisdom and spiritual attainment.

Joseph was the middle son of a wealthy Essene family. His brothers often teased him for being so pious as they were interested in making their way in the world of business. All three sons were given the very best education available at that time.

At the age of thirteen Joseph dedicated himself to the highest initiatory Order of the Essenes and a lifetime of holiness and prayer (either the Nazarene or Essene sect). He often had dreams and visions which he took seriously and acted upon.

After his twentieth birthday Joseph apprenticed himself to a carpenter in Tiberias beside the Lake of Galilee. It was the custom for devout students to spend the hours after midnight until the cock crowed in study of the Torah and prayer. He married when he was forty, as was the custom. (7.1)

Joseph's wife of forty-nine years died when James was very young. He was left with four sons: Judas, Josetos, Simon and James, and two daughters Lysia(Assia) and Lydia. Mary raised James as her own and was sometimes referred to as Mary of James. Joseph was awarded the care of Mary one year after his wife died.

The Holy Family on their journey to Bethlehem is sometimes depicted in ancient art including the teenage son of Joseph, perhaps James, leading the way. (7.2)

Another Story of Their Meeting and Courtship

Joseph's family were tradespeople. Joseph had become a carpenter. He was working on an addition to the house that Mary's parents were building in Nazareth. Mary brought a cup of water to him, and the courtship of this couple began. They were married two years later when Joseph was twenty-one years of age.

Joseph built a one-room house on a hillside on the north side of Nazareth which was to be their home. This flat- roofed structure had an adjacent barn for animals. An oven and a two-person mill for grinding grain was placed in the back yard. The furniture consisted of a low table, sleeping mats, a loom and some stools on a stone floor. In later years he built another larger room that was used as his carpenter shop during the day and for sleeping at night. Joseph and Mary were married in accordance with Jewish tradition in her parents' house in Nazareth, and then they moved into their new house. Unable to know what momentous occurrence would prevent them from living in it for a long time.(7.3)

Joseph's Angelic Guides

Ecstatic visions and angelic communications became more and more common to Joseph as the years went by. When he received the call to come to the Temple in Jerusalem, he acted immediately. As his entire life had been guided by angelic communication from celestial beings, he was the essence of piety. He was radiant with the light of illumination surrounding him. His entire life had been dedicated to God.

Both Mary and Joseph were taught the Mysteries of the Fire-Mist in the human body (Kundalini): changing negative impulses into positive to create an energy that an Initiate can use to bring the Light of Spirit into manifestation in his body. The Light is used in mental and spiritual creativity to stimulate the pineal and pituitary glands, to enter into the heart chalkra, thus enhancing the normal powers of the individual. References were made to these processes by the Church Father Hippolytus who sought to discredit them.(7.4)

Joseph's Challenges

Joseph was subject to very vivid dreams. After Mary told him of the visit with the Angel Gabriel, he was skeptical though he trusted her. The conflicting idea that a child of a human being could also be a child of divine destiny disturbed him. Joseph was afraid lest those who knew not the laws of God would misunderstand and misjudge, and he was in a quandary." (7.5)

Joseph dreamed of a brilliant celestial being The Angel of the Lord appeared unto him in a dream, saying, *"Joseph, thou son of David, fear not to take unto thee Mary thy wife: for that which is conceived in her is of the Holy Ghost. And she shall bring forth a son, and thou shalt call his name JESUS for he shall save his people from their sins."* (7.6)

Joseph struggled with the conflicting challenges that occurred as he was a very strict adherent to the Hebrew Law. However, he listened and followed the direction given him in dreams to shelter Mary from banishment or stoning for being unwed and pregnant.

Chapter 8

Honors Above and Below

Mary proved herself immune to the trials, tribulations and temptations of the world. As she passed test after test her mystical experiences increased and her spiritual faculties became more encompassing. Always under the tender guidance of her Angel teachers, she was being prepared for her next soul adventure.

The Nine Initiations of Mary in preparation for the Annunciation- called "Novenas" by the Catholic Church- were to have taken place in nine days' time. During this time the Lesser Mysteries were reviewed and the power of the Seven Creative Days as listed in Genesis also. Each day the power over that element for that day was given her. The first degree is that of Purity. The second degree is Immaculate Conception. And the third degree is the Holy Birth.

As the plan for the Christ was revealed, she was lifted into the highest heaven and robed in luminous white and crowned with many sparkling jewels, reflecting her own elevated soul body.(8.1)

During this time she was privileged to review

the vast work of the development of the human species from the androgynous time before the fall to the present time of materiality. As this was reviewed, her feelings of humility increased. To be the chosen one to birth the Christ lifted her to exultation. She was given the spiritual power over the four earthly elements symbolized as: Fire, Earth, Air and Water. These describe the process of preparation that must be made by any aspirant who desires to attain the level of initiate. Water is the symbol of work on emotions. Fire refers to the overcoming of the desire nature and earth, the subjugation of all material interests including the physical body by means of spiritual power. Air refers to the process connected with illumination of the Mind. (8.2)

At midnight of the eighth day Mary was subjected to the same test given to Solomon. She choose as he did, the highest of all possible choices.

The question was:"*Since thou hast found grace in my eyes, ask what thou wilt and it shall not be denied thee even to the half of my kingdom.*" Mary replied: "*For myself I ask nothing, but for the human race, all. Let the Messiah be born.*"

On the ninth day, again she was lifted up into the great exaltation of the heavens.

Amidst the joyous singing of the Angels she was crowned with the inscription "*Mother of the Divine One.*" This ceremony was climaxed by the coming of the great white Archangel Gabriel with his message of Annunciation. He was filled with a brilliant light like a star and with the perfume which became part of Mary's consciousness. Mary knelt in veneration before the Archangel Gabriel and, realizing her mission,began it by murmuring, "*Lord, let it be unto me according to thy word.*"(8.3)

The Immaculate Conception consists in the complete dedication of the sacred life forces on the altar of the Holy of Holies. This rite is always accompanied by celestial music and the triumphal chanting of angelic choruses. This spiritual being was the highest ever to be given to a person in a female body. The sensitization process was lengthy and strenuous even for one who was already of such a high attainment.

Those who worship the Holy Mother, worship not the person she was but the Wisdom Attribute which she exemplified.

This feminine principle is formative in its nature; consequently the Virgin became, through this Miraculous Conception, the mother of a new and higher ideal called the

Christ in the Christian world, and known by various names in other world religions.(8.3)

The result of her incarnation was to lift the patterns within the human to include the new and awakening feminine principle.

After the flood as mentioned in the Old Testament, the replenishment of the earth with human occupants allowed polygamy to readmit a larger number of souls.The purpose was quantity not quality. The respect for the feminine principle was largely lost. Many of the ancient religions still practiced today are burdened by this limitation.(8.3)

Initiations of the Virgin Mary

The First Degree of the Assumption: Initiation by Water, was bestowed on Mary for her purity. The blessed Virgin was the first person of this earth to attain the power invested in those who meet the requirements of this level of purity.

The Master Jesus, the Christ, was referring to this Degree when he said, *"Blessed are the pure in heart: for they shall see God.* (8.4) Purity is an important part in the steps of an Initiate. Initiates of the Mystery Schools were given lengthy probationary time to develop purity of body, mind and soul. Until this was

45

accomplished no further training was given. Every thought, word and deed must be on the heavenly level.

Others have gained power over water as illustrated by the Master Jesus when he stilled the waves and saved the boat. Peter found that he had the power to walk on water as well when he focused on his highest level of consciousness.

In order to prepare the Virgin Mary for her role as the Mother of the Christos, she was taught to keep her emotional nature under control and lift her consciousness above all mundane happenings. In other words, she needed to be in complete rapport with the Christ consciousness. This is why she was removed from her family home at the tender age of three years and presented to the Temple for further training. This was done with her complete permission as her schedule of many hours of prayer were uninterrupted there.

As she rested during the star lit night she often saw the cross that she had read about in the Akashic records which cast its shadow over the whole earth. (8.5)

The Akashic Records are the esoteric wisdom and history of human kind from the beginning, present time and future.

The Mother Mary occupies a prominent place as the epitome of the Degree of Purity celebrated by esoteric Christians starting the last Sunday in November and culminating on the Holy Birth Night. Contemplation of the life of the Holy Virgin is considered the first step on the pathway toward the Degree of Purity.

The Second Degree: Initiation by Fire. In order to attain to Initiation by Fire an aspirant's initial task is to bring under control all anger, hatred, envy, resentment, jealousy, lust and all other destructive emotions; these must be changed into constructive powers which transmutes the desire bodies into bodies of light. As one unfolds in spiritual understanding certain centers of the chakras are activated, which indicates the Initiate has passed the Second Degree.

The Third Degree: The Rite of Pentecost, Initiation by Air. The Initiate truly understands that All is God and that all people are one with God. Time and space are transcended, enabling the Initiate to travel at will to any place or time. The gift of doing miracles was attained by Mary and the disciples at Pentecost which was referred to as: " *the Holy Comforter, which is the Holy*

Ghost, whom the Father will send in my name, he shall teach you all things." (8.6)

The Fourth Degree: The Rite of Assumption, Initiation by Earth. Having mastered this degree one truly understands the significance of the Master Jesus' statement, *"I am the Light of the World."* Having exchanged her earthly home for her heavenly home, Mary was welcomed into the angelic realm enabling her to perceive the life and work of the Angels.(8.7)

Mary daily communed with Angels accompanied by brilliant luminosity. The experience needed no further explanation. The idea that she would be the chosen one had not entered her mind, only that she vowed to serve as the handmaid.

Early Christians honored her by calling her the *"Queen of Angels and of Men "* as well as the *"Lily of Israel."* She was called the *"Dove of Helios"* by the Essenes. (Rosicrucian)

An old story is told in the Gospel of the Hebrews, translated by Cyril of Jerusalem, that when the Christ wanted to come to earth, the Father summoned a mighty power in the heavens who was called Michael and entrusted the Christ to his care. The power came down into the world, and it was called

Mary, and Christ was in her womb for seven months. then she gave birth to him and he grew up and he chose the Apostles who preached him everywhere. (8.8) Other sources say that it was the Angel Michael who became the Christ.

Do not let this confuse you. Stories and legends being what they are, there are many ways to explain a happening.

Chapter 9

The Annunciation to Mary

It was a trying time for the Holy Family. Mary was unaccustomed to life outside of the Temple. The world she entered must have appeared very large and the people strange. Those who knew her circumstance may have ridiculed or shunned her. Her aloneness must have touched Joseph's heart.

Two years after Mary left the Temple and was living in Nazareth a counsel of the Priests decided to make a veil and other cloths for the Temple of the Lord. They called for all the pure virgins of the tribe of David. They found seven. The Priests remembered the child, Mary and sent for her. When they were assembled in the Temple of the Lord, the Priest said: "We shall cast lots for the weaving." Before him was a table filled with wool of several colors and gold thread. You shall spin and then weave the gold and the undefiled (the white) and the fine linen and the silk and the hyacinth." Mary was given the task of spinning and weaving the scarlet and purple thread She took them and went to her house. Mary took the scarlet and wove it into cloth. (9.1)

The Virgin Mary was honored by the Temple

Priests to spin the cloth for the Temple. One of the few things a woman of means was allowed to do was to spin, weave and sew. According to many references the handwork that Mary did was remarkably beautiful

The Annunciation to Mary

Mary took the purple and began to spin. She took the pitcher and went forth to fill it with water at the well, A voice said: *"Hail, thou that art highly favored; the Lord is with thee: blessed art thou among women."* (9.2)

She looked about her to see from where this voice was coming. Not seeing anyone she went back to her house, set down the pitcher, and returned to work on the purple cloth.(9.3) Coming into the chamber where Mary was the Angel Gabriel filled it with a great light. He saluted her, saying, *"Hail, Mary ! Virgin of the Lord most acceptable! O Virgin full of Grace! The Lord is with you. You are blessed above all women. You are blessed above all men that have been hitherto born."* •

Mary was well acquainted with the countenances of Angels, and the light from heaven was no uncommon thing to her. She was neither terrified by the vision of the Angel, nor astonished at the greatness of the light, but rather troubled about the Angel's extraordinary words.

Gabriel continued; *"Fear not Mary, I do not intend anything inconsistent with your vow of chastity in this salutation: for you have found favor with the Lord, because you made virginity your choice.*

Therefore, while still a virgin, you shall conceive without sin, and bring forth a son. He shall be great, because he shall reign from sea to sea, and from the rivers to the ends of the earth. And he shall be called the Son of the Highest; for he who is born in a mean or lowly state on earth reigns in an exalted state in Heaven.

And the Lord shall give him the throne of his father David, and he shall reign over the house of Jacob for ever, and of his kingdom there shall be no end. For he is the King of Kings, and the Lord of Lords, and his throne is for ever and ever."

Mary replied, *"How can that be? For seeing, according to my vow, I have never known any man, how can I bear a child without the insemnation of a man's seed?"*

Gabriel continued, *"Think not, Mary, that you shall conceive in the ordinary way. For, without lying with a man, while a virgin, you shall conceive; while still a virgin, you shall bring forth; and while a virgin you shall give suck. For the Holy Ghost shall come upon you; the power of the Most High shall overshadow you, without any heat or lust. So that which shall be born of you shall be holy, because it is conceived without sin. And when he is born he shall be called the Son of God."*

Mary stretched forth her hands, and lifting her eyes to heaven, said, *"Behold the handmaid of the Lord! Let it be unto me according to thy word."*(9.4)

The Angel read her thoughts and said: *"The power of the Holy Ghost shall come upon you and the Most High shall overshadow you without any heat or lust."* (9.5)

The Angel Gabriel had taught her to read the Akashic records (God's Book of Remembrance) where she was exhalted to find the mission of the mother destined to birth the high Master. She also realized something of the life she would endure, the misunderstanding, humiliation and even persecution involved. Mary always had the right to choose and she always chose the highest required to fulfill this task which meant that she alone must face the challenges.

The Angel Gabriel suggested she travel to Hebron to visit her cousin Elizabeth.

"And behold, Elizabeth, thy kinswoman, also has conceived a son in her old age, and she who was called barren is now in her sixth month; for nothing is impossible with God"

But Mary said, "Behold the handmaid of the Lord; be it done to me according to thy word." And the Angel departed from her.(9.6)

The incoming ego may hover around the mother-to-be for years until the right time and stays in the mother's aura for twenty-one days after conception before it enters her body to assist in building its new instrument. Every step of the body development is governed by the archetypal pattern and is chosen beforehand by the incoming ego. It can be influenced also by the surrounding emotions and happenings in the mother's life. (9.7)

The Journey to Hebron

Mary had completed the cloths for the Temple when the Angel Gabriel announced the Holy Birth. She immediately prepared to take the purple and scarlet cloths to the Temple and then journey on to visit her cousin Elizabeth in the mountains of Hebron.(9.8)

Mary was still accompanied by the Temple Virgins assigned to her as some had taken the vow of virginity following her example. It would have been unwise for a woman to travel alone or even in a group of women. It was likely that one of Joseph's sons and perhaps some of Joseph's workers accompanied them.

The journey was dangerous from Nazareth to Jerusalem, particularly for the helpless, aged, women or children. Robbers and Roman soldiers often attacked travelers, taking their belongings and assaulting them. Women were often the carriers of whatever money or jewels the family carried. A large group was safer than a lone traveler. The Essenes had established rest places or Hospices, some built in caves, along the main roads in order to assist the travelers. Mary often stopped to help those in need and was much appreciated by them. (9.9)

Roman Soldier Story

Roman soldiers were stationed along the way to keep the peace and to remind the people of their power. One group of soldiers was resting on the road to Jerusalem. Mary's group had to pass that way. The noise of the soldiers laughter grew louder and louder as they approached. Fear seized the hearts of the travelers. But as they came into sight instead of becoming louder, their voices became quiet. Somehow a light effused from Mary's group that brought a feeling of peace and awe to those Romans standing by, and they did nothing. It is said that those soldiers were affected for some days with an experience of peace. (9.10)

On reaching Jerusalem, Mary presented the exquisite purple and scarlet cloths she had made. The Priest admired her fine work and blessed her saying,

"Mary, the Lord God has extolled your name and so you will be blessed by all the generations of the earth." (9.11)

Chapter 10

The Insemination of the Christ Ego

Therefore the Lord himself shall give you,
a sign; Behold, a virgin shall conceive, and
bear a son, and shall call his name
Emmanuel. (10. 1)

Mary knew all that would transpire; it was foretold in the books of the Hebrews and the Akashic records. She was conscious of the preparation and the changes taking place in her body to receive a Holy Infant of a much different vibratory level. Her own vibrational level had to be elevated. It was understood by the Angel Gabriel that Mary would benefit from being with Elizabeth in the quiet mountainous area where peace and harmony would surround her and condemning voices would not reach her. (10.2)

As this occurred a greater awareness of the sacred life forces was revealed to her and she became totally dedicated to the action of Spirit.

The Magnificant, cerebrated by the Catholic Church, reflects this moment in eternity.

"And there appeared a great wonder in heaven;

a woman clothed with the sun, and the moon under her feet, and upon her head a crown of twelve stars: And she being with child cried, travailing in birth, and pained to be delivered. And she brought forth a man child, who was to rule all nations with a rod of iron: and her child was caught up unto God, and to His throne. and the woman fled into the wilderness, where she hath a place prepared of God...And to the woman were given two wings of a great eagle, that she might fly into the wilderness, into her place, where she was nourished for a time. (10.2)

Essene Grottos

The Essenes operated certain rescue houses or hospices. Some of these were grottos below the ground. Some contained as many as twenty rooms. Usually, they were well hidden from marauders. All were well lighted by oil lamps hung from the ceiling, free from moisture, heat or cold. Many were very comfortable inside with furniture, wall decorations and fresh water was provided. Volunteers, nurse-midwives lived nearby to aid anyone who needed help.

Mary most likely passed one of these on her journey to visit Elizabeth. *"It was to the Essene grotto near Bethlehem that Joseph and Mary went for the birth of the child."* (10.3)

Mary Enters Elizabeth's Door

And {she} entered into the house of Zacharais
and saluted Elizabeth. And it came to pass,
that, when Elizabeth heard the salutation of
Mary, the babe leaped in her womb; and
Elizabeth was filled with the Holy Ghost:

And she spake out with a loud voice, and said,
"Blessed is the fruit of thy womb. And whence
is this to me, that the mother of my Lord should
come to me? For, lo, as soon as the voice of thy
salutation sounded in mine ears, the babe
leaped in my womb for joy...."

And Mary said, "My soul doth magnify the Lord.
And my spirit hath rejoiced in God my Savior.
For He hath regarded the low estate of his
handmaiden: for, behold, from henceforth all
generations shall call me blessed. For he that
is mighty hath done to me great things; and
holy is His name."

And Mary abode with her about three
months, and returned to her own house. (10.4)

According to the writings of Schonau, Mary
explains to Elizabeth how she was
impregnated by God, "The Lord did with me
what a musician does with his harp. The
musician sets and tunes all the strings so that
they give forth a sweet and harmonious

melody, and then he sings while playing on it.
Thus God brought into harmony with His will
my soul and heart and mind and all the senses
and actions of my body. And being trained in
this manner by His wisdom, I used to be
carried by the Angels to the bosom of God the
Father, and there I received such consolation
and joy, such bliss and well-being, such love
and sweetness, that I no longer remembered
that I had ever been born in this world.
Besides, I was in such close intimacy with God
and his Angels that is seemed to me as though
I had always existed in that true glory. Then
when I had stayed there as long as pleased
God, the Father, He gave me back to the
Angels, and they carried me back to the spot
where I had begun to pray.

When I found myself on earth again and
recalled where I had been, this memory
inflamed me with such a love of God that I
embraced and kissed the ground and stones,
the trees and other created things, out of love
for Him who had created them. And it seemed
to me that I should be the handmaid of all the
Temple-women, and I wished to be subjected to
all creatures, out of love for their supreme
Father. And I frequently had this experience.
Once when I was thinking that I never wanted
to be deprived of God's grace, I arose and went
to read in the Scriptures, desiring something to
console my soul. When I opened the book, the

*first thing I saw was this passage of Isaiah,
"Behold a virgin shall conceive and bear a
son." As I understood from this that the Son of
God was going to choose a virgin to be His
Mother. I immediately resolved in my heart, out
of reverence for this virgin, to remain a virgin
myself and to offer myself to her as a handmaid and always to serve her and never to
leave her, even if I had to travel all over the
world with her." (10.5)*

Another discription of the insemnation comes
from the Rosicrutian records.

*"Fear not! I come to bring thee a message of
great joy, for thy day hath come to fulfill the
prophecy of the Magi. Thou hast found favor
with God and thy Bretheren, and now thou
shalt conceive from the word of God."*

*And when Mary heard this she disputed,
saying: "Shall I conceive from the word of God?
And yet shall I bear as every woman beareth?
And the voice of the figure said: "Not in the
manner of thy understanding shalt thou bear.
... The word of God shall be breathed upon
thee and its power shall make thee holy and
bless the seed that is of God. Wherefore, that
Holy life which shall be born of thee shall be
called the Son of God and he shall attain the
name Jesus because he shall be the God in
man and will become the God with men."*

Mary answered, " It shall be according to the word of God!" (10.6)

Mary's high level of attainment made it possible for her to adjust to the higher frequencies needed to be impregnated by the Holy Spirit.

The four main events that stared her life are the Rite of Annunciation, the Rite of Immaculate Conception, The Rite of Pentecost and the Rite of Assumption. Mary came to earth to prepare not only for the coming of the Lord Christ but also to prepare the way for pioneers who would usher in the new Christian Dispensations. These four Initiations are the Initiation by Water, Fire, Air and Earth. Those who would enter into their mysteries must first overcome the conditions resulting in disease, old age and death. (10.9)

Instructions for Mothers to Be

The awaiting soul may follow the prospective mother for years looking for the perfect time for it to come forth. After conception, the incoming soul remains in the aura of the mother for a short time--about twenty-one days. Then it enters her body and begins the work of developing its new vehicle. The prospective mother will benefit greatly by living in harmonious surroundings and holding inspirational thoughts. Enjoying nature or anything that can uplift the heart is beneficial.

The new form is built conforming to the archetypal pattern in the higher realms which are set into motion by the emerging ego according to previous lives upon earth. Mary was able to assist the Master Jesus in building the most perfect of bodies.

Negative forces of evil, disease and destruction create inharmonious patterns that externalize as homely features, and weak or distorted bodies.

Constructive forces of peace, sympathy, helpfulness and love build harmonious lines that favor healthy, beautiful and peaceful individuals. No person ever enters this life alone nor exits this life alone. We are always surrounded in God's love and blessings.

Chapter 11

Zecharias, Elizabeth and John the Baptist

Luke begins his narrative with the priest Zecharias and his wife Elizabeth who was barren until an advanced age. To the Hebrews their being barren meant that they were out of favor with God.

Each priest was responsible to give at least one week of service every six months to the Temple. Each day they drew lots for their responsibility of that day. Zacharais task this day was to offer incense upon the golden altar which was a great privilege.

"And it came to pass, that while he executed the priest's office before God in the order of his course, according to the custom of the priest's office, his lot was to burn incense when he went into the Temple of the Lord. And the whole multitude of the people were praying without, at the time of incense. And there appeared unto him an Angel of the Lord standing to the right side of the altar of incense. And when Zecharias saw him, he was troubled, and fear fell upon him.

But the Angel said unto him, "Fear not

Zacharais: for thy prayer is heard; and thy wife Elizabeth shall bear thee a son, and thou shalt call his name John. And thou shalt have joy and gladness; and many shall rejoice at his birth."(11.1)

The Angel Gabriel appeared to Zecarias as he performed his duties at the Temple. The ceremony of presenting the offering of incense on the golden altar in the Holy Place during the time of prayer is a description of building of the soul body, the Golden Wedding Garment, which was woven of deeds of love and service.

Zecharias was given fore knowledge, seeing the prophet Elias returning to earth, who prophesied thus:

"And he shall go before him in the spirit and power of Elias, to turn the hearts of the fathers to make ready a people prepared for the Lord. (11.2)

And Zecharias asked, *"How can I be sure of this? I am an old man and my wife is along in years."*

And the Angel said, *"I stand in the presence of God, and I have been sent to speak to you and to tell you this good news. And now you will be silent and not able to speak until the day this happens because you did not believe my words, which will come true at their proper time."(11.3)*

It was Zacharias privilege to prepare a physical body for the use of this great spirit on his earthly mission. When one is privy to the secrets of Initiation he must always remain silent to those waiting without, but the strange radiance that is revealed in his aura is clear for those who have eyes to see. It is not at all unlikely that from that day forward Zecharias shone with a noticeable light that caused his murder as being the suspected father of the Messiah.

"And the people waited for Zecharias, and marveled that he tarried so long in the Temple. And when he came out, he could not speak unto them: and they perceived that he had seen a vision in the Temple: for he beckoned unto them, and remained speechless.

And it came to pass, that, as soon as the days of his administration were accomplished, he departed to his own house." (11.4)

Elizabeth conceived and for five months she stayed in seclusion filled with joy and gratitude. She said,

"The Lord has done this wonderful thing for me. In these days he has shown his favor and taken away my disgrace among the people."(11.5)

John the Baptist's Immaculate Conception was announced by angelic annunciation prior to that of Jesus the Christ to his Mother Mary.

The Master Jesus praised the spiritual status of John when he said, *"Of all that is born of woman, there is none greater than he."*

Mary may have stayed with Elizabeth until after the birth of John which would explain why she knew the details of his conception, Zacharais' dumbness, and his naming him. In later years she must have been the one who related the story to Luke who wrote about it so completely.

After a lifetime of preparation, his ministry was only about six months in duration.

Chapter 12

Mary Visits Elizabeth

Mary knocked on Elizabeth's door and called her name. When Elizabeth heard Mary's voice, she tossed aside the scarlet thread which she was spinning and ran to the door and opened it. She blessed Mary and said,

"Blessed are you among women, and blessed is the child you will bear! but why am I so favored, that the mother of my Lord should come to me? As soon as the sound of your greeting reached my ears, the baby leaped for joy."(12.2)

The moment of arrival was beautifully explained by Luke. At the time Mary entered Elizabeth's garden and greeted her, Elizabeth was awarded new insight and spoke with a loud voice

"And Mary said, My soul doth magnify the Lord, and my spirit hath rejoiced in God my Savior." (12.3)

These words reveal that the mother-to-be, Mary, realized her mission in preparing for the incoming Christ. Her higher illumination was clearly revealed from her research in the

Akashic Records and her recognition that she was the woman clothed with the Sun, standing with her feet on the Moon as described in the Akashic Records. Mary may have thought previously that Elizabeth was the virgin who was to conceive.

Mary spent six inspiring months with Elizabeth residing in her inner sanctuary. It was a soul-call from their intended sons to prepare for their incarnating that awakened the latent spiritualized powers in Mary and Elizabeth. All had been prepared before the mothers' births to provide the perfect vessels possible for the incoming Masters.

Mary's memorable visit with Elizabeth must have occurred rather soon after her conception as Elizabeth was in her sixth month. Mary stayed with Elizabeth until after the birth of John.(12.4)

The sanctuary of the hill county was a sacred retreat for both women as they read the Akashic records and communed with the Angels. Mary occupied Elizabeth's shrine room during her visit and as the incoming soul of the Master-ego was developing in her body, she walked with greater light and her words were more illumined than ever before as both women prepared with their incoming Masters the highest, most perfected bodies possible, reaching spiritual heights of beauty and joy.

This stage of Initiation occurs in the body of the neophyte as she becomes conscious of the higher frequency of vibrations.The Miraculous Conception of Mary consists of the complete dedication of the sacred life force to the One God. When this occurs it is accompanied by the singing of the angelic choruses. Mary's song continues:

"For he hath regarded the low estate of his hand maiden; behold, from henceforth all generations shall call me blessed. He that is mighty hath done to me great things; and Holy is his name." (12.5)

The spirit who was to be John the Baptist was already aware of his surroundings in his mother's womb, and he also recognized the spirit of Mary and greeted her with great joy.(12.6)

Birth of John the Baptist

Mary and Elizabeth both knew their sons before birth and as the true Masters that they were, they accepted their roles as the chosen mothers with joy and dedication to God.

Now Elizabeth's full time came that she should be delivered; and she brought forth a son. And her neighbors and her cousins heard how the Lord had showed great mercy upon her; and they rejoiced with her.

And it came to pass that on the eighth day they came to circumcise the child; and they called him Zacharais after the name of his father.

And his mother answered and said, Not so, he shall be called John. And they said unto her, "There is none of thy kindred called by that name."

And they made signs to his father, how he would have him called. And he asked for a writing tablet, and wrote saying, His name is John.

"And they marveled. Zacharias' mouth was opened immediately, and his tongue loosed, and he spake and praised God." (12.7)

Day by day Mary's womb kept swelling. She became frightened; returned home, and hid from the people of Israel. She was just sixteen years old when these mysterious things happened.(12.8)

The people who heard about this wondered what is this child going to be? For the Lord's hand is with him. (12.9)

Zacharias returned to Jerusalem to fulfill his Temple commitment. Herod kept close watch over the occurances of the people lest they revolt. Zacharias previously strange behavior did not go unnoticed.

Chapter 13

Joseph Returns

When Joseph returned from his building business, Mary was six months pregnant. Upon entering his house and seeing her pregnant, he was shocked and threw himself to the ground on sackcloth and began to berate himself.

"What kind of an excuse can I present to the Lord God? How can I pray on her behalf? I received her a pure virgin from the Temple of the Lord God and didn't stay here to protect her. Is this trap for me? Someone has done this evil deed in my own house. Someone has lured this virgin away from her promise and violated her? The story of Adam and Eve has been repeated in my house. Adam was praying when the serpent came, and finding Eve alone, deceived her, and corrupted her." (13.1)

Joseph called Mary and said to her,*"How could you have done this? You were special in God's sight. Have you forgotten the Lord your God? You have brought shame on yourself. You were raised in the Holy of Holies and fed by the hand of an Angel from on high."*

Mary cried bitter tears. *"I'm innocent. I have not been with any man."*

And Joseph said to her,"*Where did this child you are carrying come from?*" She could not answer.

Joseph spoke no more, and went into the field.

He pondered what he should do. Should I hide her? and go against the law of the Lord. Should I disclose her condition to the Temple and let them handle the matter? I don't know what they will do. What if the child is heaven-sent? I would end up handing innocent blood over to death. So what should I do with her? I know: I'll leave her quietly. (13.2)

That night as he was sleeping a messenger of the Lord appeared to him in a dream and said: "*Fear not, Joseph. Do not be afraid of this young girl. The child in her womb is of the Holy Spirit. She will give birth to a son and you will name him Jesus--the name means savior of the people.*" Much relieved, Joseph got up from his sleep and praised the God of Israel who had given him this blessing. Then he began to protect the girl." (13.3)

Annas the scholar came to visit him and said to him,"*Joseph, I have missed you at our assembly.*"

And he replied to him, " *I was just too tired from my journey.*"

Mary came out of the door and Annas saw her. He ran to the High Priest and said to him,

"*Remember Joseph? the man from Nazareth, who you vouched for. And gave to him the Temple Virgin, Mary? He has committed a serious offense against God.*"

And the High Priest asked, "*What has he done?*"

Annas replied."*Joseph has violated the virgin Mary who you trusted him with protecting. He has gone in unto her and hasn't notified anyone of his action. He is keeping her hidden.*"

" *Are you sure Joseph has done this?*"

Annas replied, "*Send the Temple officers and you'll find Mary pregnant.*"(13.4)

And so the Temple assistants went and found Mary pregnant. They brought Mary and Joseph to the court.

"*Mary, what have you done?*" the High Priest asked her. "*You have humiliated yourself?*

Why did you forsake the Lord your God? You, who were raised in the Holy of the Holies and fed by Angels of the Lord. You, who heard their hymns and danced for them."(13.5)

And she wept with great sadness: *"As the Lord God lives, I do not know. I am innocent. Believe me. No man has come in unto me."*

The High Priest said accusingly,*"Joseph, what have you done? Tell us the truth, now!"*

And Joseph said,*"I swear, as the Lord lives, I am innocent in this matter."*

And the high priest said, *"Tell the truth! You've violated this virgin of the Temple and haven't disclosed this action to the people of Israel. You have married her privately. You must adhere to the law so that your child shall receive the blessing of the people of Israel."* Joseph said nothing.

The High Priest said, *" You will return the virgin as she was, pure and undefiled to the Temple!"*
" And Joseph gave a loud cry."

The High Priest decreed, *" Today, you will drink of the Lord's bitter potion and we shall see who is lying."* And so Joseph drank the cup of bitter potion and was sent into the wilderness for the night, but he returned healthy with no ill effect.

And the High Priest made Mary drink the potion and she was sent into the wilderness apart from Joseph for the night. She also came back healthy looking. (13.6)

Not satisfied: The High Priest decided that the test would be given using radiant water. Then their auras would manifest the color of sin. Each was given the radiant water and then they were placed in a darkened room. A group of Priests observed them. Nothing but pure Light came from then.(13.7)

So the High Priest said, *"Since the Lord God has not exposed your sin, then I cannot condemn you."* And he dismissed them as pure in heart and clean in body.

So, Joseph and Mary returned to Nazareth, celebrating and praising the Lord God of Israel. (13.8)

Chapter 14

The Holy Birth

King Herod died in 4 B.C, according to
Josephus and other outside sources. The
census mentioned in the Gospel of Luke,
claimed that Jesus was born just before the
world-wide census conducted in Syria, may
have been in 6 C.E. which would have been
after the birth. On the other hand this
census may not have been as far reaching as
world-wide and may not have been the
reason for the Holy family to travel to
Bethlehem.(14.1)

The Romans were wise enough to know that
if the Jews were to revolt against them the
leaders would be from the ruling class, the
House of David, most likely.

"Mary was of the house of David and required
to enroll in Syria, the Roman province in
which Palestine was located. Women twelve
years of age and older were required to pay a
poll tax and therefore had to register."(14.2)

"The day came when Joseph found it
necessary to journey with Mary to avoid
censure from the local devout community
because of their predicament. (14.3)
It would be inconceivable for Joseph to start

off on a journey, without adequate funds. The Jews, used to being captives, carried their jewels with them as insurance. They often sewed money or jewels into the hems of their garments. Mary and Joseph would not return to replenish their funds for three years. Although Joseph was not the biological father Jesus was considered to be his legal son as he was born under Joseph's responsibility.

And it came to pass, that there went forth a decree from the Emperor Augustus that all the Jews should be taxed, who were of Bethlehem in Judea: (14.4)

Joseph said to himself, "I will take care that my children be taxed: but what shall I do with this young woman? To have her taxed as my wife I am ashamed; and if I tax her as my daughter, all Israel knows that is a lie. When the time of the Lord's appointment shall come, let the Lord do as is fitting.

And he saddled the ass, and put Mary upon it, and Joseph, James and Simon followed after her. (14.5)

Jerusalem was a three day journey from Nazareth, and Bethlehem was twelve miles beyond. Joseph was leading the way and turning about saw Mary sorrowful, and said within himself, perhaps she is in pain from that which is within her. Later, when he turned about again he saw her laughing, and said to her, *"Mary, how does it happen that I sometimes see thee sad and sorrowful and later laughing and joyous."*

Mary replied to him, *" I see two people with mine eyes, the one weeping and mourning, the other laughing and rejoicing.* (14.6)

Later as Joseph led them along the road, Mary said to him, *"Please take me down, for that which is within me presses to come forth."*

Joseph replied, *"Whither shall I take thee for this place is desert? I see no place to hide thy shame."*(14.6)

Then Mary said again to Joseph, *"Take me down, for that which is within me mightily presses me."*

Joseph took her down, and he found there a cave, a hospice and led her into it. (14.7)

According to the Rosicrucian records Mary arrived three days before the birth and the Magi were already in the vicinity of Bethlehem, also awaiting the hour.

When the star appeared in the heavens at its highest apex and then began its rapid decent, the Magi knew that the day had come.

The Mystical Story

And leaving Mary with his sons in the cave, Joseph went forth to seek a Hebrew midwife in the village of Bethlehem. Soon he saw a woman coming down from the mountains, and she said, *"Where art thou going, O man?"*

And he said to her, *"I go to Bethlehem to inquire for a Hebrew Midwife. Mary fell to my lot as my ward and is not my wife.*

She asked, *"Where is the woman that is about to be delivered?"*

"She is in the cave." He answered. *"It is Mary, who was educated in the Holy of Holies, in the house of the Lord. She has conceived by the Holy Spirit."*

The midwife asked, *"Is this true?"*

"Come and see." The midwife accompanied him.

As they were going, they looked up and saw that the clouds were motionless. The birds of the air had stopped in the midst of their flight.

They looked down and saw a table spread, and working people sitting around it, but their hands were upon the table, and they did not eat. All their faces were motionless, fixed upwards.

Then they beheld the sheep dispersed, and yet the sheep stood still. And the shepherd lifted up his hand to smite them, and his hand continued up. And he looked at the river, and saw the lambs with their mouths close to the water, and touching it, but motionless. They did not drink."(14.8)

As they stood in the entrance of the cave a bright cloud overshadowed them, and the midwife said, *"This day my soul is magnified, for mine eyes have seen surprising things, and salvation is brought forth to Israel."*

As Mary knelt in prayer, she was absorbed in ecstasy.

From time to time she levitated above the earth, lost to the sight of Joseph and the midwife. The glorious light surrounded her and extended like a bridge of gold from heaven to earth. Angels walked down this bridge singing until the air was filled with the shimmering of their auras and their song of triumphant canticles. Twelve lights illumined the cave. Though Mary's physical body was seen, her consciousness was in the higher realm where she was given the babe. Then It became visible to those watching. (14.10) The twelve lights representing the latent centers within each person remained within the mother and child.

For a few moments everything stood still. Then in unity everything and everyone went on with what they had been doing.(14.11)

Enveloped in the luminous glory of hosts of triumphant Angels and Archangels heralding the glad New Day of women's emancipation and chanting mighty hosanna for the coming Master Mary, the perfect Type-Pattern of the New Age, was caught up in clouds of light to welcome, without anguish or physical pain, the incoming of her Divine Son. (14.12)

The cloud changed and became a great light in the cave. Their eyes could not bear it. As the light gradually decreased, and they could see the infant appear, sucking at the breast of his mother Mary.

The midwife cried out, *"How glorious a day is this. Mine eyes have seen this extraordinary sight."*

As the midwife went out, another midwife met her. And the first midwife, Zalome, said to her, "*Salome, I will tell you a most surprising thing, a virgin hath brought forth a child. You know that is contrary to nature.*"

Salome replied, "*As the Lord my God liveth, unless I receive proof of this matter and stretch forth my hand and examine her, I will not believe this.*" Salome went in and she said, "*Mary, show thyself, for a great controversy is risen concerning thy virginity.*"

And Salome examined Mary, but her hand began to burn and wither and she groaned bitterly with pain. "*Woe be to me, because of mine iniquity; for I have tempted the living God, and my hand is ready to drop off my arm.*"

Salome prayed begging the Lord's forgiveness. An Angel of the Lord standing by Salome said, "*The Lord God hath heard thy prayer. Reach forth thy hand. Take the child, and carry him, and by that means thou shalt be restored.*"(14.13)

Salome went to the child and touched him. And immediately she was cured. Filled with great joy, she knelt and worshiped him, and said, "*This is a great king which is born to Israel.*" (See picture Insert)

Salome went out of the cave, being approved by God. A voice came to Salome's ears

"Declare not the strange things which thou hast seen, till the child shall come to Jerusalem." Salome departed carrying her secret with her. (14.13)

The first midwife, Zalome, who witnessed this birthing still had work to do. Bringing a basin,water and some salt, she bathed the babe in the traditional manner of the Hebrew Law. Tradition requires that every baby born to Jewish parents be bathed immediately with salt to cut the waxy residue of the womb and stimulate the child's skin.

The postnatal bath was considered a sacrament in the Greco-Roman world. The postnatal bath of Alexander the Great was recalled as an important ritual of his life. After the salt bath the babe was washed with sweet smelling water.

After the bath, the midwife wrapped Jesus in swaddling cloths that Mary had brought with her and presented him to his earthly mother.

Swaddling cloths were made of a cotton gauze strip perhaps twelve feet in length and about eight to twelve inches in width which were wrapped around and around the new born. (Dr.Rocco Erico)

As Zalome was leaving, carrying the bath water, a child covered with leprosy came up to her and asked that she pour the bath water over her. The midwife did as requested, and the child was made whole. This healing announced the special properties of the Holy Babe's bath water which was used numerous times in later stories.

Esoteric Stories

On that first magical Holy Night a golden light encircled the whole world. Angels and Archangels with luminous voices praised the Holy Family as they descended to earth. As they mingled with the humans they were visible to some who were highly elevated in consciousness. A golden ray swept Mary out of sight when the Holy Babe was given to her awaiting arms.(14.14)

It was necessary that the babe be born in Bethlehem as Bethlehem signifies the spiritual level of attainment.This has been a recognized power place since the earth began.

At the stroke of midnight, surrounded by a luminous aura the Holy Babe was born. Every Initiate must also leave Nazareth, the material life, and make the journey to Bethlehem, the purified life.

Joseph knelt a short distance from Mary and gazed upon this scene with profound awe. Tenderly, he fashioned a simple manger, lined it with sweet hay and laid a blanket upon it in preparation for the babe.

Outside the cave were beasts, mainly cattle, sheep and some donkeys. All was still according to the legends. Even the turtle doves did not utter a sound that night. (14.15)

The Star (Angel Gabriel, some believed) shone brightly over the cave lifting the entire vibratory rate of the planet in preparation for the incoming Spirit.

From about ten p.m. until midnight on Dec. 24, the sign of the virgin (Virgo) was on the horizon of the eastern sky, while the three stars of Orion, the sign of the Three Magi were gleaming brightly in the western sky. (14.16)

All the earth paused in this holy moment. The birds stopped mid flight, The sheep near water did not drink. The cattle in their stables fell upon their knees. All nature responded to this hallowed time.

Chapter 15

The First Visitors

When an old lame Hebrew woman was passing the cave and saw Joseph looking intently into the cave, she went in.

And behold, the cave was filled with lights, greater than the light of lamps and candles, and greater than the light of the sun itself. Her eyes could hardly see. An infant was wrapped in swaddling cloths, and sucking the breast of his mother Mary.

When her eyes could see, The old woman asked Mary, *"Art thou the mother of this child?"*

Mary replied, Yes, she was. On which the old woman said, *"Thou art very different from all other women."*

Mary answered, *"Since there was not any child like my son, so neither is there any woman like his mother."*

The old woman answered and said, *"O my Lady, I am come here that I may obtain an everlasting reward."*

Then Mary, said unto her, *"Lay thine hands upon the infant;"* When she had done this, she became whole.

As she started to go out of the cave, she said, *"From henceforth, all the days of my life, I will attend and be a servant to this infant."* The old Hebrew woman saw all these miracles and she gave praises to God. And said, *"I thank thee, O God, thou God of Israel, mine eyes have seen the birth of the Savior of the World."*(15. 1)

The events of the holy night continued. When the shepherds came they made a fire, and they were exceedingly rejoicing, The heavenly host of Angels appeared to them, praising and adoring the supreme God.

The shepherds were Initiates of the Temple able to see and hear the Angels. The cave at that time seemed like a glorious Temple. Angels and men united in songs of praise to adore and magnify God, on account of the birth of the Lord Jesus.

Who were these shepherds who were keeping watch? There were hundreds of shepherds watching their sheep at night because this was mainly a sheep-raising area.

The center of spiritual power "Bethlehem,"was guarded over by the Raim (seeing ones, or Initiate-Shepherds).

Spiritually-awake these Initiates were the guardians of the Temple sheep who possessed extended powers of clairvoyance and clairaudience as they saw and heard the Angel messengers. This Holy Night was the opening of the way to free humans from the Wheel of Life, the curse of birth and death, instigated by Adam and Eve in the Garden of Eden

The tidings of great joy brought heightened energy throughout the entire world and opened the path for whoever will to partake of the Water of Life freely. The chant of *"peace on earth, good will toward men"* was sung at a particularly high vibratory level, bringing greater ease to humanity releasing more brotherhood, altruism and peace than ever before broadcast to the earth.(15.2)

Actually, the Master Jesus, the Christ, cares little that we celebrate his birth except that it provides an opportunity for humanity to become open to higher levels of consciousness and brings about a greater vibrational level to the earth.

A shepherdess prepared a room for them in Bethlehem where Mary, Joseph and the babe, rested until the day came to dedicate the babe at the Temple in Jerusalem. (Jesus returned to visit that generous shepherdess in Bethlehem before he started his mission.)

Mary longed to see Elizabeth so Joseph sent word to Zacharais and Elizabeth saying *"The babe is born."* (15.3)

The Circumcision Performed

And when eight days were fulfilled for his circumcision, his name was called Joseph.The Angel predicted that the name Jesus would be given him later in life.(15.5) His family may have called him Jesus while Joseph was still alive.

On the eighth day when the time of his circumcision had come, according to Hebrew Law the child was circumcised while they were still living in Bethlehem.

Jesus used the name Joseph in primary school and when he was a student at Mt. Carmel College, and also in his later journeys.

Circumcision is traditionally done on the eighth day to all male babies born to the Jews. It may have been performed in Bethlehem by Zacharais himself as he was qualified, if he was alive at that time.

The rite of circumcision has a more exhalted

meaning when it is done on the Higher level. It symbolizes the complete subjection of the lower man. In the case of Jesus of Nazareth attending Angels presided over this rite singing hosannas of praise extolling the Master who had come to earth for this great mission. Other Angels descended on a ray of light bearing ribbons of light. The sound echoed and reechoed throughout the highest expanse of heaven.

Mary was always so in tune with her blessed son that she felt the physical pain and also understood the joy and homage paid him by the heavenly host. (15.6)

The old Hebrew woman still attending the Holy Family, took the foreskin and/or the navel-string and preserved them in an alabaster box of perfumed oil.

She had a son who was a herbalist, to whom she said, *"Take heed, do not sell this alabaster box of spikenard ointment. It is very valuable. Even if you are offered three hundred pence for it"*

Years later, this was the same alabaster box which Mary, sister of Lazarus procured, and poured forth ointment upon the head and feet of Jesus, then wiped it off with her hair.(15.7)

Laid Him in the Manger

Another story relates that on the third day
after the birth of our Lord Jesus Christ, Holy
Mary went out from the cave, and went into
the stable and put her child in a manger,
and an ox and an ass worshiped him. Then it
was fulfilled that which was said through the
prophet Isaiah: 'The ox knows his owner and
the ass his master's crib.' (15.8) This was
commonly done when the baby was born in a
dark place as getting the child used to
sunlight was important.

Being human, Jesus reveals the possibilities
of human attainment. That which he did, all
may do. Had he come in any other form, he
would not have been the supreme example,
but the great exception. Jesus, Mary and
Joseph set the example that those who aspire
to the high level of Initiate may emulate. This
is the Truth that this story wishes to teach.
They were showing the way for all the people
of the earth to follow.(15.9)

Chapter 16

Dedication at the Temple

The Law of Moses ordains that every male which opens the womb shall be called holy unto God and must be presented on the fortieth day from birth at the Temple in Jerusalem for dedication.

After ten days Mary and Joseph brought the babe to Jerusalem, and on the fortieth day from his birth they presented him in the Temple before the Lord, making the proper offerings for him. At that time two turtle doves were the proper offering to be made. (16.1)

The pair of turtle doves offered by Joseph and Mary were believed for centuries to indicate that they were poor. Others have said that those were just a token gifts to the Temple. At that time offerings were mostly in the coin of the realm, fruit or flowers.

There were other families waiting for the Priest to bless them. When High Priest Simeon, who took Zachariah's place after his murder, entered the room, he saw rays of light shining around the Holy Family. He instantly recognized their high calling as it is said he saw a pillar of light eminating from them and they were accompanied by a band of Angels guarding over them.

And he came by Spirit into the Temple: and when the parents brought in the child Jesus, to do for him after the custom of the law. He took the babe in his arms, and blessed God, and said,"Lord, now lettest thou thy servant depart in peace, according to thy word; for mine eyes have seen thy salvation, which thou hast prepared before the face of all people: a light to lighten the Gentiles and the glory of thy people Israel."

Joseph and Mary marvelled at those things which were spoken.

And Simeon blessed them, and said unto Mary, his mother, "Behold, this child is set for the fall and rising again of many in Isarel: and for a sign which shall be spoken against; (yea, a sword shall pierce through thine own soul also) that the thoughts of many hearts may be revealed." (16.2)

Simeon may have been a singer and/or an Essene serving in the Temple as he is described as a sincere and earnest worshiper of God who kept the Law in spirit as well as in letter. Because of their advanced degrees in consciousness of both Simeon and Anne, the former teacher of Mary, were allowed to attend the dedication ceremony.

Anne gave thanks to God and blessed the Master as God's gift to the salvation of Israel. Anne may have been a poetess and Mary's teacher and surrogate mother during her time serving at the Temple: it was especially meaningful to Mary that she be present and recognized at the dedication ceremony. (16.3)

Baby Jesus Spoke

The following account we found in the book of Joseph the high priest, called by some Caiaphas. He relates, that Jesus spake even when he was in the cradle, and said to his mother: "Mary, I am Jesus the Son of God, that word which thou didst bring forth according to the declaration of the Angel Gabriel to thee, and my Father has sent me for the salvation of the world." (16.4)

Chapter 17

The Wise Men Came

And it came to pass, according to the prophecy of Zoradascht, (Zoraster) that wise men (perhaps not three.) (17.1) traveling from Tarsus, Arabia and Sheba brought with them offerings: gold, frankincense, myrrh and the Scripts of Adam, and worshiped him offering their gifts.They also presented the babe with a rare pendant to wear indicating his high accomplishments. (17.2)

The star that led the Magi from afar must have begun its orbit months before the Holy birth as the wise men came from the east of Judea. It was said that the first sighting of the star held a picture of a child bearing a cross. And that the Magi saw the image of a mother and babe residing in a lowly place which assisted them in recognizing the Holy family. (17.3)

The Star

The star which was their guide in their journey; the light of which they followed till they returned into their own countries. (17.4)

Johannes Kepler (1571-1630) observed the conjunction of Jupiter and Saturn in 1603 and determined that it was possible that Jupiter and Saturn may have been in conjunction in 7 BCE.

The study of astrology was used in that time by royalty to foretell their future and astrologers were considered the wisest of the realm and often held high positions at court. Four duplicate cuneiform scripts impressed into clay that may have been Balthassar's Almanac, an amazingly rare find from ancient Babylonia and inscribed dating to 8 B.C.E,predicted three conjunctions of Saturn and Jupiter during the year 7/6 B.C.E, in the constellation of Pisces. The new year began at the vernal equinox March/April. The three conjunctions were in May, October and December. The scripts indicates that at the December conjunction Mars had also moved into Pisces.

If the Magi came from Babylon it would have been at least a two-month journey. If they left at the second sighting, they would have arrived just as or about the time of a December first birth date.(17.5)

Justin Martyr (who died C.165) interpreted the Magi as having fulfilled the Old Testament prophecy regarding the Messiah as predicting that "before the child knows how to call 'my father' or my mother,' the wealth of Damascus and spoils of Sumaria will be carried away by the king of Assyria." He believed that the Magi were pagan worshipers and at the crib was the moment of conversion when they renounced their pagan practices.

Tertullian in his writings later suggests that the fact that the Magi left by another route was their way of demonstrating their change to a belief that Jesus was the Messiah.

Pope Leo wrote in his sermons on the Epiphany: It was not just the star that attracted their eyes, but the rays of truth also penetrated their hearts, so that before they started on their toilsome journey, they first understood that the One who was promised was due the finest gifts of gold as royalty, incense as divinity, and myrrh as a mortal....and so it was of great advantage to us future people that this infant should be witnessed by these wise men." (17.5)

Other scripts hold that the star was the Angel Gabriel leading the way to the Holy Child. It may have been up to four months before the Magi found the babe. (17.6)

Some held the story of the Magi as having been foreseen in the Psalm 72:10-11. "May the kings of Tarshish and of the Isles render him tribute, may the kings of Sheba or Seba bring gifts,.. May all the nations serve him." To some this implied an international acceptance by the whole world.(17.7)

Astrologically speaking from about ten p.m. until midnight of December 24, in northern latitudes, the sign Virgo, the Virgin, the sign of purity of the Immaculate Conception was to be seen on the eastern horizon about the time of the holy birth. In the belt of Orion three stars shone signifying Magi who heralded the glad tidings of the Nativity. (17.8)

According to Urantia, the conjunction occurred on August 1st at noon 7 BC and the conjunction of Jupiter and Saturn occurred on May 29, 7 BC, on September 25 and December 5 of that same year. (17.9)

Who Were the Magi?

The three wise men were: Caspar, an Aramaic name sometimes spelled Gadaspar, advanced in age, with long white beard, king in Tarsus. His gift was gold which represents the dedication of spirit and possesses the highest vibratory power of all metals.

The King of Arabia, was often depicted as clean shaven, a youth by the name of Melchior (an Aramaic name meaning "The king is my light") gave frankincense, which represents the body, a symbol of the spirit's most impermanent vehicle.

Balthasar, was an African or Moor, depicted with a long brown beard. Balthassar, taken from the Greek, means "O Lord, protect the king," the dark king came from the land of spices and gums, Seba or Sheba. He brought myrrh which is the symbol of discipleship, the purpose of life or the impermanence of life on the physical plane.

The fourth gift given by the Magi was the testament scroll which Adam, the first man, created and delivered to his son Seth. Many years later presented to the Holy Family, It is said that Jesus presented it to the Temple when it was time for him to start his mission.(17.10)

Mary took one of Jesus' swaddling cloths in which the infant had been wrapped, and gave it to them as a gift with her blessing. They considered it among their greatest treasures.(17.11)

The earliest depiction of the Magi is in the oldest catacombs or sarcophagi. Later depictions were displayed in public places to inspire the faithful. Many times the Magi were dressed in shorter robes than was traditional in Israel, with pointed hats pointing skyward to the stars. (17.12)

The momentous event, the Holy birth,was hailed by many Initiates in many lands. The Magi and many others were given the knowledge of the child who was to become the king of the world. With great joy the Magi set out on a dangerous journey to find the babe. The constellation of the mother and the child shone brightly in the heavens. The mysterious Star, under the direction of the Archangel, the Christ, guided them night and day.

They read the story in the Akashic Records and did not expect to find the babe in Herod's palace. It was already known to them to look in a humble place. When they entered the room the celestial beauty of the child and his Mother was overpowering, and they prostrated themselves. The picture was identical with their visions they had seen in the Eternal Scrolls.(17.14)

Upon returning to their own lands the Magi met with those who had sent them or were knowledgeable in these matters, who were eager to hear of their journey. Kings and princes and other wise men came from far and near. According to their tradition they built a great fire and held a feast to give an accounting of their experiences.

Then they brought forth the swaddling cloth which Mary had given them and cast it on the fire. The fire appeared to consume it. But when the fire died, the cloth was unharmed. The fire did not touch it. Then they began to dance about with joy and kiss it and to put it upon their heads and their eyes, saying, *"This is certainly a surprising thing. The fire could not burn it,"* The Magi took it, and with the greatest respect put it among their treasures. (15.40)

Years later, the disciple Thomas traveled to the Indies and found these same wise men teaching and carrying the New Light far from Judea. He labored with them. They were finally put to death by their own people.

The story continues that their remains were discovered by Empress Helena, mother of Constantine, and after lengthy travels, were brought to Constantinople. Later, they were taken to Milan and found their final resting place in the Cathedral at Cologne. Over each skull is inscribed in red rubies their names and the symbol of Christianity, the cross.

Greater gifts were given to the Magi on the other side: to Caspar, who gave the golden cup was given spiritual riches. To Melchoir, who gave the bowl of frankincense, was given greater faith. And to Balthasar, who gave the gift of myrrh was given truth, meekness and understanding of the eternality of life. All are the necessary qualifications for Initiation.

The gifts of the Wise Men represent the body, soul and spirit, and their dedication to the Master Jesus. The bitterness of pain and sorrow, before the lower nature of the Initiate has been transformed, is represented by the myrrh. Frankincense represents the transmutation of the soul. And spirit refines all lower nature and eventually transmutes all into gold.

The path of Transmutation for the neophyte sometimes called Initiation is exemplified by the wise men and symbolizes the cleansed desire nature and the spiritualized mind, which is the highest teaching of the Mystery Schools.

It is reported that the Magi returned to their kingdoms, sold all their earthly goods and preached the teaching of the Christ.

A few years later there was a congregating of all the wisest living on earth held at the library at Alexandria. Jesus of Nazareth attended and to his delight the youngest of the three Magi also attended. (17.16)

From the esoteric point of view, the reason why Jesus was born in Bethlehem is that there is a magnetic center between Jerusalem and Bethlehem through "which powerful spiritual currents are passing into the center or the heart of the earth." This holy place was being prepared for thousands of years for this very occasion. All that came before in the evolutionary cycle of men and their religions were in preparation for the coming of the world Savior, the Christ.(17.17) Even as a babe the Master was proclaimed the Christ. Of course, this was not honoring the human individualization of Jesus, but the level of attainment, Master, that he entered this life already having attained.

The Feast of Epiphany

The Mystery Schools in which the Magi were teachers, continued the celebration of the Holy Days during the first month of each new year. The events of the life of the Christ child for the Initiates of the Mystery School represent the steps on the Way of Attainment towards Initiation.

The four weeks of Epiphany begin on the first week in January. The focus of the first week is on prayer and meditation. St.Paul was said to recommend, "Pray without ceasing. Pray even while performing daily duties. During the evening hours review the day and the year just passed and rededicate oneself to a better, more noble year ahead. This evaluation directs one toward a more spiritual plan for the upcoming year."

The second week one pays attention to the desire level to transmute into purity and bring about a clearer degree of vision.

The third week centers on self-discipline of the mind, learning to discriminate the higher from the lower, the greater from the lesser. This brings all levels of consciousness into the higher level of spirit.

During the fourth week the degree of purity is to be developed in the Christ mind, which inhabits all people.

The Mystery Schools taught the Initiate to bring about the Christened man who thirsts and hungers for the things of the spirit, to understand the Master Jesus' statement, "I have meat to eat that ye know not of."

The eternal quest symbolized by the Knights

Templar of the middle ages, who sought the Holy Grail was developed within the Initiate as the realization of the meaning of the passage "Seek ye first the kingdom of God and his righteousness and all these things shall be added unto you."
(17.18)

Chapter 18

The Essenes, Elizabeth, Zacharias and John

Only the highest spiritual attainment permitted the priest of Zacharias' time to present the offering of incense on the golden altar in the Temple during the time of prayer. It was when Zacharias was engaged in the performance of this sacred rite that the Angel of the Annunciation appeared before him. The ceremony of presenting the incense on golden altar during the time of prayer is a veiled description of the building of the soul body, the Golden Wedding Garment, which is woven of the sublimated essence of deeds of love and service performed by the aspirant.

John's was an Immaculate Conception preceeded by an angelic Annunciation. Zacharias means "God's remembrance," and Elizabeth, "God's oath."

Zacharias, through great spiritual illumination, was enabled to look into the future beyond the veil of physical worlds of time and space, all is an eternal here and now. In these high realms Zacharias saw the prophet Elias returning to earth and he prophesied thus: "And he shall go before him in the spirit and power of Elias, to turn the hearts of the fathers to the children, and the disobedient to the wisdom of the just; to make ready a people prepared for the Lord." (18.1)

Zacharias saw furthermore that is was to be his great privilege to prepare a physical body for the use of this great spirit during its mission upon earth. It is an experience that will always cause the recipient to stand out from the average person. A strange radiance suffuses his aura; his words, both spoken and written, possess a vibrancy of life that eludes adequate description as they are charged with higher meaning.

King Herod

Herod was an astute though evil governor. He made note of any change in leadership of the Temple. He heard of Zacharias strange behavior. When the Magi came asking for the whereabouts of the babe born to be King of the Jews, he remembered Zacharias. Herod became angry that there were being born claiments to his throne. He called his guards and sent them to Bethlehem to slay all male children under three. And they did.

The evil forces most active at this time were concentrated in the court of Herod. Both the White and Black witchcraft were practiced. Herod had two motives in slaying the innocents: first, he wanted to frustrate the work which the Spiritual Hierarchies were endeavoring to consumate through the work of Jesus and secondly, it was a means of procuring, for his evil purposes, the vital essence of purity from the blood of the innocent victims.

Other guards found Zacharias on the steps of the Temple having just completed the service for the day. They said, "The king demands that you tell us where your son is. He answered, " I am the minister of God, a servant in the Holy Place, How could I know where they have taken him?" After the first meeting with Herods soldiers, Zacharias sent word to Elizabeth to flee.(18.2) Herods plot to kill Jesus and John had reached Elizabeth's ears and she fled with John to the mountains.

When Elizabeth heard that they sought John, she took him up into the hill country above Hebron, looked about her where she could hide him: and there was no hiding place she could find. She groaned and said with a loud voice:"*O mountain of God, receive thou mother and a child.*" Elizabeth was not able to go any further. The mountain opened and took them in. An Angel of the Lord was keeping watch over them and there was a light shining always for them in the cave. (18.3.)
For the third time Herod angrily ordered his

guards to, "*Go back and tell that wily priest that he is in my hand; that if he does not tell the truth, does not reveal the hiding place of John his son, then he shall die.*"

Again Zacharias answered, "*I can but give my life for truth; and if the king does shed my blood the Lord will save my soul.*"

Now Zacharias stood before the altar in the Holy of Holies engaged in prayer. A guard approached him with a dagger and thrust him through; he fell and died before the curtain of the sanctuary of the Lord.

And when the hour of salutation came, for Zacharias daily blessed the priests, he did not come. They did not find his body, but they found his blood turned into stone, and they were afraid, went out and told all the people that Zacharais had been slain. The grief of the people engulfed the land of Israel and they lamented three days, three nights.(18.4)

After the three days the Priests held a council about whom they should appoint in Zacharia's place and the lot fell to Simeon.

Elizabeths high level of communication with Mary and Joseph warned them as well. Later, when the Holy family passed near the place where Elizabeth and John were hiding, they met on the spirit level with joy. Elizabeth and John accompanied by Angels, leading and preparing the way to a place of safety where no persons lived.

When Mother Mary heard of Herod's edict she laid Jesus in a manger and covered him with straw to hide him from the soldiers. It was said that only a few babies were slain. Perhaps only twelve as Bethlehem was a very small village.

Now it was Simeon to whom it had been revealed by the Holy Spirit that he would not see death until he had seen the Christ in the flesh." (18.5) It was Simeon who blessed the Holy Family at the Temple

After hiding for quite a time, Elizabeth took John out of the mountain to a place where they could view the entire city of Jerusalem. She related the story of his father's bravery and murder cautioning him not to seek revenge as that would lead him away from his divine mission.

Chapter 19

The Journey to Egypt

And when they were departed, the Angel of the Lord appeareth to Joseph in a dream, saying,"Arise, and take the young child and his mother, and flee into Egypt, and be thou there until I bring thee word: for Herod will seek the young child to destroy him."

When he arose, he took the young child and his mother by night, and departed into Egypt: and was there until the death of Herod: that it might be fulfilled which was spoken of the Lord by the prophet, saying, "Out of Egypt have I called my son." (19.1)

Instead of going directly to Egypt to be safe from Herod's legions, the Holy Family hid in a crevasse in the mountains and remained there until it was safe to leave. As they traveled they found small groups of Essenes who sheltered them knowing of the work destined for the Holy Child. They were always protected by the angelic hosts.

It was an especially difficult journey. The way was hot. Not a breath of cool air or water to drink. The Holy Family paused to rest by a large outcropping of rock that afforded them some shade. As they rested, a child came as if from nowhere wearing tattered rags in advanced signs of leprosy. He joyously greeted them as if he had been awaiting their coming. They saluted him kindly and asked the way from him. He invited them to his village (a robber hideout). They followed him through the rocks and soon came to a small village where he introduced his mother.

On seeing the babe in Mary's arms, she immediately offered water to bathe the child. After Jesus was washed, Mary washed his clothing. The leprous child begged to be washed in the leftover water. Mary complied and the child was completely cured of leprosy. Such joy filled that village. The Holy Family stayed the night and the next day were led through the most dangerous parts of the journey by appreciative villagers. (19.21)

The Lion and the Ox Shall Eat Straw

Further along the way, they were met by some lions, leopards and wolves. Mary was afraid but the animals bowed down their heads and accompanied them showing them the way. Jesus smiled on her and she was reassured. To hold their belongings they had brought a cart pulled by oxen. None of their animals were harmed.

Thus was fulfilled the prediction of peace, *"The wolves shall feed with the lambs, the lion and the ox shall eat straw together."* (19.3)

The Palm Tree Story

Mary, Joseph and Jesus had been traveling for three days when they came to a date palm orchard. It was hot and they were running short of water so they rested in the shade. Mary gazed up into the tree high overhead and saw ripe dates. We must have some, she thought. Calling to Joseph who was searching for water nearby, she told him of her desire. He saw how impossible the request was and discouraged her, saying they must look for water instead as they were nearly out and must care for their animals.

Jesus commanded the palm tree to bend down so that his mother could get some dates to eat. And the tree bent to her feet. When all had had their fill, Jesus released it and commanded the tree to give them some of the water under its roots. A beautiful gurgling spring manifested with enough water for the travelers, and some for the next day.

They rested the night there, and the next day when they were leaving, Jesus gave a special gift to the palm tree.

"I give thee this privilege, that one of thy branches shall be taken by my Angels and planted in my Father's garden. And henceforth all who win contests shall be told that they have won the palm of victory."

An Angel came and plucked a branch from the palm tree and flew away with it. All present fell down in fear, but Jesus reassured them.

Joseph said that since it was so hot that they would travel along the seashore, but Jesus was impatient and said that he was tired of traveling and wanted to be in Egypt right away. And as he spoke they saw the hills of Egypt coming into view.

One day they were walking through a field of wheat about to be harvested. They picked some of the wheat, ground them and toasted them on the fire. They were delicious. From that time on that field yielded much more wheat than they took. Jesus was two years old when he entered Egypt.

They found lodging in the house of a widow as they entered Egypt and lived there for a year.

One day Jesus was playing with the neighbor children that he had been watching. They had a dead fish that had been lying in the yard for some time. Jesus brought a basin of water and commanded the fish to move and it did. Then he commanded the fish to let go of the salt in it. It did. Then he commanded it to jump into the basin; it wiggled and finally leapt into the basin. The neighbors saw this and told the widow woman with whom they lived, and she made them leave. (19.4)

And The Idols Fell

After they left the widow, the Holy family were seeking lodging near a well known shrine in another town.The priest often interpreted the wisdom given by the idol to those who worshiped there.

Near to that idol was the inn of the town, into which Joseph and Mary had stopped to rest.

In every place the Holy family visited the idols fell. A concerned group of magistrates and priests were meeting before one of . Egypt's greatest idols to discuss the matter. The high priest asked the idol, *"What is the meaning of all this worry, and dread, which has fallen upon our country?"* The idol answered them, *"The unknown God is come; nor is there anyone besides him who is worthy of divine worship; for he is truly the Son of God."* And then the idol fell down, The inhabitants of the city were astonished about the idol and rushed to the shrine leaving the Holy family alone in the lodging.

This High priest had a three year old son, who was possessed by great multitude of devils, who uttered many strange things. When the devils seized him, he walked about naked with his clothes torn, throwing stones at everyone.

The possessed child went into the inn where Joseph and Mary were resting and found the swaddling cloths of Jesus where Mary had hung them to dry on a post. He took one of them, and put it on his head.

The devils then began to come out of his mouth, and fly away in the shape of birds and serpents. The boy began to sing praises, and give thanks to the Lord who had healed him.

When his father saw him restored to health, he said, *"My son, what has happened to thee? By what means were thou cured?"* The son answered, *"When the devils seized me, I went into the inn, and there found a woman with a little boy, whose swaddling clothes she had just washed and hung out to dry. One of these I took and put upon my head, and immediately the devils left me, and fled away."* The father rejoiced, *"My son, perhaps this boy is the son of the living God, who made the heavens and the earth. For as soon as he came amongst us, the idol was broken and all the gods fell down, and were destroyed by a greater power."*

The prophecy was fulfilled which saith, Out of Egypt I have called my son. (19.5)

The Robbers Flee

Joseph and Mary fled from Egypt for their lives when they heard that the idols had fallen down and were destroyed. They were seized with fear and trembling, and they remembered that when they were in the land of Israel, Herod, intending to kill Jesus, slew all the infants in Bethlehem. They did not doubt that the Egyptians; if they heard that their idols been had broken, fallen down, would come after them and burn them with fire.

That night they went along the road where the robbers lived who stole from travelers as they passed by and left the victims bound. As the robbers were celebrating their stolen booty, the robbers and their victims heard a great loud noise like a wealthy king was marching with his troops in their direction with drums, chariots and bugles. The robbers became frightened and ran away, leaving all they had stolen. The captives untied each other and gathered all their goods together to leave.

When the Holy family came to that place, they were asked, *"Where is the great king? We heard a great king coming this way. When the robbers heard the loud sound of an army marching down the road, they left. We have escaped."*

Joseph said, *"He will come."* And they all went their way puzzled, but rejoicing at being freed from the robbers. (19.6)

The Demented Woman

A few days later they came to another city where there was a deranged woman who was said to have been attacked by Satan when she had gone out for water at night. She could not bear to wear clothes or live in a house. When they bound her with ropes and chains she broke them and ran away into the desert. She stood at the crossroads and threw stones. When she saw Mary she stopped. Mary saw her and pitied her. Immediately the woman smiled. The dementia was gone. A demon left her saying, *"Woe to me, save me from you, Mary, and your son."*

The woman returned to her home and dressed herself. She told her father who was

Mayor of the city how she had met this lady at the crossroads who healed her.

Her family and friends came together in celebration and honored the Mary and Joseph. (19.6)

The Deaf and Dumb Bride

The next day the Holy family left with many gifts and provisions for their journey. That evening they arrived at another town where a wedding was being celebrated. The bride was deaf and unable to speak. Caused, it was said by sorcerers and Satan.

The Holy family entered the town on their cart pulled by oxen. Mary was riding, holding her son as they came. The bride saw them and rushed up to them with her arms outstretched to hold the child. Mary let her hold him as she got down from the cart. The bride embraced him and kissed him and rocked him back and forth. Immediately she was able to speak, and as Mary spoke to her, she was able to hear. That night a great celebration of thanks to God was held because the bride had been restored to health.

The little town believed that God and his Angels had done this miracle. In this place they abode three days, meeting with the greatest respect and most splendid entertainment.

And being then furnished by the people with provisions for the road, they departed.(19.7)

The Woman With the Serpent

In another city a woman went down to the river to bathe when the cursed Satan leaped upon her in the form of a serpent and stayed upon her night and day, This woman asked Mary if she could hold the infant. Mary consented. As soon as the woman held the child, Satan left her and slithered away.

The same woman brought perfumed water to wash the Lord Jesus; when she had washed him, she preserved the water. And there was a young girl there named Isis, whose body was white with a leprosy, who after being sprinkled with this water, was instantly cleansed from her leprosy.

The people agreed that without doubt Joseph, Mary, and Jesus were gods, for they do not look or act like mortals.

When they were making ready to go, Isis, who had been troubled with leprosy, asked to accompany them. They consented, and she went with them to a city, in which there was a palace of a great king.

The Healed Princess

They stayed at an inn in this city near the palace. Isis desired employment and went to the prince's wife. She found her in a mournful condition, and asked the reason for her tears.

The wife replied, *"I am under a great misfortune, of which I dare not tell to anyone."*

"If you will entrust me with your secret, perhaps I may find you a remedy for it." Isis replied.

"Isis, you must promise to keep the secret, and not uncover it to anyone alive."

"I will!" She promised.

The princess said, " *I have been married to the prince, who rules as king over large dominions, and lived a long time with him, before he had a child by me. At length I conceived. But alas! I brought forth a leprous son.* "When the prince saw him, he said to me, *"Either kill him, or send him to some nurse in a far away place, that he may never be heard of. And now take care of yourself; I will never see you again."*

"Alas, my son! Alas, my husband! I have disclosed it all to you."

Isis replied, *"I have found a remedy for your misfortune, which I promise you will succeed, for I also was leprous, but God hath cleansed me. The child who is called Jesus, the son of Mary, has cleansed me."*

The woman inquired where this Jesus was of whom she spoke. Isis answered. *"He lodges with you in this same inn."*

"But by what means, were you cleansed from your leprosy? Will you tell me?" She was getting interested.

"The water with which he was washed, was poured upon me, and my leprosy vanished."

The prince's wife then arose and in their tradition provided a great feast for Joseph among a large company of men.

The next day she took perfumed water to wash the Lord Jesus, and afterwards poured the same water upon her son, whom she had brought with her, and her son was instantly cleansed from his leprosy.

Then she sang thanks and praises unto God, and blessed is the mother that bare thee, O Jesus!.....

She then gave very large gifts to Mary, and sent her away with the great respect.(19.8)

Chapter 20

Other Stories

The Bewitched Brother

The next day they came to the outrskirts of a city they saw a woman and her two daughters by a certain grave weeping in a cemetary. Mary saw them and sent Isis who was traveling with them to inquire of them what the matter was. She went to them and asked, but they made no answer so she asked, "Who are you and where are you going to stay as night is approaching?" She explained that they were travelers seeking a place to lodge for the night.

The three women invited them to lodge in their house. They came to a new house, well furnished with all sorts of furniture. More than they were accustomed to in their homeland and the Holy family were well situated. Coming into the parlor to stay out of the winter weather, Isis found the three women still weeping. Standing beside them was a mule covered with a silk cloth and an ebony collar around his neck, They were kissing and feeding the mule.

Isis said, *"What a handsome mule."* Through their wailing the women said, *"This mule, was our brother, born of the same mother as we. When our father died he left us a very large estate, we had only our brother to go in and out for us and do our business. We procured a suitable wife for him as we thought he should be married as other men and he fell under a spell of a woman who bewitched him.*

Early one morning while the doors were still shut fast, we saw that our brother was changed into a mule as you see now. We became in this sad condition in which you see us, having no father and no brother. We have sought assistance of many wise men, magicians, and diviners, but they have been to no avail.

When we find ourselves overcome with grief we go to our father's tomb. When we have cried sufficiently, we return home."

When Isis heard this, she said, *"Take courage, and cease your tears, for there is a remedy for your afflictions near at hand in your house. Go to my mistress Mary and tell her your secret. Beseech her to be compassionate in your case."*

The women went to Mary, and sat down with her. *"Lady Mary, pity us your handmaids, for we have no head of our family. No father, or brother to buy our food at the market or manage our business."*

And they told Mary their story. We entreat you to return our brother whole to us.

Mary was sympathetic to their situation, and set Jesus upon the back of the mule. Saying to her son, *"Jesus, please restore this mule to his true shape of a man of reasonable nature as he was before."*

The mule immediately changed into human form, and became a young man again.

Such rejoicing! The family were rejoined. And they worshipped Mary and Jesus. Lifting the child upon their heads they danced about. They sang, *"Blessed are you and thy mother, O Jesus, O Savior of the world! Blessed are the eyes which are so happy to see this miracle you have done."*

Then the sisters said, *"Our brother is restored to his former self by the help of the Lord Jesus, and the kindness of Isis, who told us of Mary and her son. Since our brother is still unmarried, it is fitting that he marry Isis."Are you willing to marry our brother?"* Isis agreed.

When they consulted Mary in this matter, she gave her consent. The joyous family made a splendid wedding for Isis and their brother.

Afterwards they glorified and praised God,

saying, *"O Jesus, son of Mary, you changed our sorrow into gladness, and mourning into mirth!"*

Joseph and Mary rested ten days, then went on their way. When it was time to leave, there was much weeping, especially by Isis who had been healed of leprosy. (20.1)

The Dragon Story

Four children were traveling with Mary, Joseph and the babe, Jesus. They were suffering in the heat of the day when they came to a cave and decided to rest a while. Mary dismounted from the wagon and found a comfortable rock to sit on in the cave. Jesus was in her lap when suddenly dragons came out of the cave, breathing hard and threatening them Everyone jumped back in fear. Jesus got down from his mother's lap and stood before the dragons, And they bowed down and worshiped him. Mary called him back, but he said, *"Fear not, Do you not remember that though I am a child, I am and always will be the perfected man. It is expected that all the beasts of the forest grow tame before me. They will not hurt us."*

Thus the fulfillment of the word,*'Praise the Lord out of the earth, ye dragons and all deeps,'* And no one was harmed. (20.2)

More Robbers

The people warned them about the robbers
who lived ahead of them in the desert so
Joseph and Mary decided to cross by night.
Traveling by night was good as it was cool
and the moon was full so they could see the
way clearly. As they moved along they saw
two robbers lying in wait by the side of the
road. Behind them there was a large camp of
robbers who were sleeping.

When Joseph saw them It was too late to turn
back. They were caught. One of the robbers,
Titus saw that this family was special and
said to the other robber, Dulmachus, " Let
these people go. Our gang has not heard
them. Do not make the alarm." But
Dulmachus refused.

"I will give you forty drachmas and my belt,"
Titis said. *" If you will let them pass."*

Mary was listening to the kindness that Titus
was trying to do for them. Finally, Dulmachus
agree. Jesus said to his mother, *"Thirty years
from now, the Jews will crucify me at
Jerusalem and these two robbers will be raised
upon the cross along with me. Titus will be on
my right and Dulmachus on my left. As we go
to Paradise, Titus will lead the way."* Mary
replied *"God keep this path from you."* (20.3)

Three Hundred Sixty Five Idols Fall

When they came to the city of Mermopolis, called Sotinen, there was no lodging available so they stayed the night in the Temple where stood 365 idols, statues of gods.

As Mary and Child entered, all the idols fell into dust. Thus Isaiah's word was fulfilled. *"Behold the Lord shall come upon a light cloud and enter into Egypt, and all the gods made by the hand of the Egyptians shall be moved before his face."*

The Governor Affrodoshus heard of the plundering of the temple and came with his priests and guards,who expected him to punish the Holy Family. When he saw how they had fallen into dust, he worshiped the Child. *"If this were not a greater God than our gods, they would not have fallen. Bow down and worship him as our gods have done or we shall be in danger of great destruction as fell upon the Pharaoh long ago, who died with all his army in the sea."*

Then all the people bowed down and worshiped Jesus.(20.4)

The Years in Egypt

They proceeded on to Memphis, and saw the

Pharaoh, and abode three years in Egypt. The Lord Jesus did very many miracles in Egypt, which are not found in the Gospel of the Infancy nor in the Gospel of Perfection. (20.5) The journey traveling through Egypt was a long and arduous three hundred miles. The flight into Egypt was not mentioned in Luke as it was considered the call to the sense life. Each neophyte has to go though a period of probation and testing to reach the levels of Initiate, and the Holy Family was no exception.

When the Holy Family entered Egypt it is said that all temple idols fell from their shrines indicating that power of the Master Jesus in overcoming all that had gone before.

According to mystic legends, the Holy Family passed most of the time in Matariah, a town near Cairo, almost in the shadow of the Sphinx and the Pyramids. It was reported that they lived for a time with a prince called Eliajar Lazarus in Syric History.

Joseph was commissioned to make a chair for a notable personage.When it was finished, it was clear that it was too small in width. The person was much too wide in girth. Upon seeing the situation, Jesus took the two arm-rests and pulled them apart, thus widening the chair. The commissioner was well pleased and paid handsomely.

Several families fled to Egypt from Herod at the same time so there was a small group of Galileans residing in the area. The parents of Bartholomew, the future disciple, were among them.

Bartholomew was very sick and his mother was afraid he would not live. She begged Mother Mary to give her the bath-water that she had used for Jesus and his swaddling cloths. After bathing Bartholomew in the water he became well immediately. This news traveled fast. Many mothers requested the same for their sick children. (20,2)

Jesus was an apt student advanced beyond his years. Mary and Joseph spent much time instructing Jesus in the Torah, the Law and Prophets.The traditions or dogmas of the Jews were of great concern to Jesus and he had many questions. Jesus always wanted to honor the higher Law rather than the lesser. Jesus learned to read and write at his mother's knee.

In his hours of daily communion with God the Father, it was Jesus' wish that his mother remain with Him. Legends quote him as saying: *"My mother will remain with me always as the vessel and model of all perfection."* (20.3)

The years in Egypt were productive of much good. The quiet abode of the Holy Family soon became a shrine where illness of body, mind and spirit found alleviation. Joseph, with his carpentry,and Mary's skill in fine weaving and needlework provided the physical necessities.The hours from midnight to dawn were times of heavenly communion and angelic visitation. The child Jesus had communed mystically with His mother from her birth. Jesus always addressed Joseph as "my father." (20.3)

In the early stages of spritual development the aspirant will often experience a "flight into Egypt," or a slipping away into darkness. The inner life will be temporarily veiled. This can bring on an agony of spirit. But if the aspirant persists in his efforts to regain the light he will again tread the Path as was taken by the Holy Family. According to the Rosicrucian mystic, Max Heindel, *the only failure is in ceasing to try."* (20.4)

Chapter 21

Time to Return

Now Herod sat upon his throne; he did not seem to move; his courtiers came; the king was dead. His sons reigned in his stead.

When Herod died, an Angel of the Lord appeared in a dream to Joseph in Egypt, saying, "Arise, and take the young child and his mother, and go into the land of Israel: for they are dead which sought the young child's life. (21.1) Other stories claim that Mary had the dream.

When Holy family came near to Judea, Joseph was afraid to enter though Herod was dead. Archelaus his son was the new king and was purported to be worse than his father.

After days of travel they came to Bethlehem. They found many children very sick and dying with distemper.

A woman who had a son at the point of death, brought him to Mary.

"O, Mary," she pleaded, *"Look at my son. He has great pain. I fear he shall die."* Mary instructed her, *"Take a little of this water in*

which I have washed my son and sprinkle it upon him."

The woman sprinkled it upon her son who was so wearied with his violent pains that he had fallen asleep; When he awakened he had recovered.

Mary said to the grateful mother, *"Give praises to God who hath cured thy son."*

A neighbor woman of the first lady heard of the miracle brought her sick son whose eyes were almost shut as if he were dying. When she sprinkled her baby with the bath water he was restored to his healthy state.

Mary suggested she give thanks to God for the recovery of her son's health and to tell no one. (21.1)

News travels fast in a small village such as Bethlehem. Many mothers came with their children including two wives of one man, who each had a sick son. The wife called Mary came with her sick son Caleb pleading that her son be healed.

"O Mary, accept this beautiful carpet of mine, and instead of it give me a small swaddling cloth to heal my son."

The Immaculate Conception
Murillo   1617-82

Anna and Joachim Meeting at the Golden Gate.
Italian artist Giotto (600 CE)
State Hermitage Museum, St. Petersburg

The Annunciation by Rodger Van Der Weyden
The Metropolitian Museum of Art

The Nativity by Robert Campin (1425)
Salome - Midwife questions Mary's Virginity

The Adoration of the Shepards
(1485) by Domenico

Adoration of the Kings
by Gerard David

Sistine Madonna - Raphael

Assumption of the Virgin
1560 Titian

When she arrived home, she made a coat for Caleb of the swaddling cloth. After putting on the little coat, his disease was cured; but the son of Una the other wife died.

Because Mary's son lived and Una's did not a disagreement arose between the two wives. It was the family custom to alternate buying for the family each week.

Mary, the mother of Caleb was heating the oven to bake bread in the outdoor oven, and went to get the meal. She left her son Caleb playing by the oven. The other wife, Una, seeing Caleb by himself, picked him up and cast him into the oven, which was very hot, and then went away.

Upon her return to the oven Mary opened the door and saw her son Caleb lying in the oven laughing. The oven was quite cold as though it had not been heated. She knew that her rival Una had thrown him into the fire.

She brought him to Mother Mary, shaking with fear as she told her the story. Mother Mary said, "Be quiet. Be wise in this matter."

A few days later Una, the other wife, was drawing water from the well, saw Caleb play-ing by the well, and seeing that no one was near, took Caleb, and threw him into the well.

Later some men came to fetch water and they found the boy sitting on the surface of the water. They drew him out with poles, and were amazed that the child was unhurt.

Mary, Calebs mother took him once again to Mother Mary, angrily saying, *"O Mary, see what Una hath done to my son. She cast him into the well. I do not question that one time or other she will be the cause of his death."* Mother Mary replied to her, *"God has protected Caleb and God will vindicate you."*

A few days later Una came to the well to draw water and entangled her foot in the rope. She fell headlong into the well. They who ran to assist her found her skull broken, and bones bruised. So she came to a bad end. In her was fulfilled that old saying: they digged a well, and made it deep, fell themselves into the pit which they prepared.(21.2)

When they were living in Bethlehem the daughter of a prince was sent by a woman who had been healed of leprosy by Mother Mary with many assurances that she too would be healed. The child was possessed by an evil spirit When Mary had heard her story she gave her a little of the bath water with which she had bathed Jesus and one of his swaddling cloths. Before she returned home, the child was healed. (21.3)

Chapter 22

Growing Up In Nazareth

Nazareth was a life-shaping education for the young Jesus as it was located at the crossroads of the great trade road bringing many caravans to Jerusalem. He spoke and read Hebrew, Aramaic and Greek. At a very young age he was exposed to several other languages as he often asked questions of the travelers stopping to rest. He assisted his family in repairing saddles,which was one of their businesses along with carpentry.

Most families also had vineyards and raised sheep. Joseph's son, James managed the family saddle repair business and taught Jesus to do it also. Jesus was skilled with his hands and did fine work.

When Jesus was five, he loved to play at the ford of a rushing stream near their home. He would dam the flowing water creating ponds and made the water instantly pure by a single command. He shaped the soft clay into twelve sparrows. Some of the other boys made figures of other animals. Each trying to exceed the other,

Jesus, said to them, *"I shall make them walk."* And immediately they did. Then he commanded them to drink and they did. Finally, he commanded them to fly away, and they did. They did all this on the Sabbath day.

When the boys arrived home, they related to their parents the things Jesus had done. A neighbor father heard this story and told his children to beware of Jesus as he was a sorcerer. He went to Joseph, saying, *"Your boy was at the ford and took mud and fashioned twelve birds with it. He has violated the Sabbath. You know it is unlawful to play, work or do anything but read and pray on the Sabbath."*

Joseph went to the stream, and found Jesus, *"Why are you doing what's not permitted on the Sabbath?"*

Jesus clapped his hands and shouted to the sparrows: *"Be off, fly away, and remember me, now that you live!"* And the sparrows flew noisily away. They went in twelve directions, signifying the twelve disciples' mandate to go into the world and preach the gospel to every nation.(22.1)

The next day, the son of the neighbor, Annas the scholar, took a willow branch and drained the water that Jesus had dammed up. Jesus became angry, saying to him,

" You fool! What harm did the ponds of water do to you? From this moment you will dry up like the clay, and you will never produce leaves or bear fruit." Instantly the boy completely withered away and Jesus went home

The parents of the boy who had withered away picked up their son and were carrying him to Joseph and accused him, *"It's all your fault. Why did you come back here? Your boy did this."*(22.2)

Later Jesus was walking through the village when a boy ran by and bumped him on the shoulder. Jesus got angry again and said to him,*"Your journey in this life is over."* Suddenly the boy fell down and died instantly.

The village people saw what had happened and said, *"Where has this boy come from? Everything he says happens, and a child dies."*

The parents of the dead boys came to Joseph and blamed him, saying, *"Teach your boy to bless instead of making a curse. We can't have him living here. He's killing our children!"*

So Joseph called Jesus into the house. He said,
"Anger is a bad thing. It is time you learn to

control it. Why are you doing this? These people are suffering. By your word you have killed two boys and the neighbors hate and harass us. They want us to leave. You must stop this."

Jesus said, "I know that the words I spoke are not good words. I'll be still for your sake. But people must take their punishment." There and then, his accusers became blind.

The neighbors who saw this became very fearful and did not know what to do. All they could say was, "Every word he says, whether good or bad, has become true--a miracle!"

When Joseph saw that Jesus had done even more by his word, he got angry and grabbed Jesus' ear and pulled very hard. Jesus became infuriated with Joseph. Jesus replied, "Don't you know that I don't belong to you? Don't upset me more."(22.2)

The accounts of Jesus displaying disrespect to his teacher and/or killing his neighbors children show that his parents were busy getting him out of trouble.(22.3)

Many of the childhood acts of Jesus were remembered because of past predictions or later developments. Some of the language resembles his later years.

Preparation for Great Tasks

Great souls still have the human level to overcome in being prepared for a world mission. They need direction, peace and quiet to bring their spiritual powers into full fruition. Jesus' home in Nazareth provided such an environment. As time passed he learned to control himself and was able to enjoy the peacefulness of his surroundings. (22.4) Mary and Jesus' Angelic teachers brought this peaceful atmosphere and were always in tune with their pupil.

The white houses of the village were scattered among orchards of figs, olives, and pomegranates. Flocks of white doves circled overhead, and from the heights above one could see the soft shimmer of the Sea of Galilee. Knowing the companionship of pure, chaste, Initiate parents, and under the constant guidance and instruction of bands of Angels, the boy Jesus was well prepared to become a suitable instrument for the Christ to whom he was later to surrender His body.

As Hebrew parents, Joseph and Mary were expected to teach the traditions of their faith to their children at home before they started school. From Joseph, Jesus received his strict training in the Jewish tradition and acquaintance with the Hebrew scriptures.

From Mary, he received a broader view of religious life and a more liberal concept of spiritual freedom. Joseph made several attempts to enter Jesus into school that were unsuccessful. (22.5) .

The early education of Jesus progressed and soon his vast fund of knowledge became a constant source of wonder to His teachers. He was sent to what we would call elementary school on three different occasions to learn to read. The teacher always assumed he did not know the alphabet and started him at the beginning. Zechariah, one of the teachers wrote out the alphabet letters for him. Jesus proceeded to explain the esoteric meaning of each which Zechariah was unprepared to discuss. (22.6)(See Glossary for Hebrew School Systems)

The Dyer Story

Mary was noted for her fine needlework, and it was also mentioned that she was weaving when the Angel Gabriel came to her announcing the Holy Birth.

One day Mary went to the dyer, the son-in-law of Joseph to commission some of her woolen yardage to be dyed. Lysia, married a man who was a dyer by trade, named Salem,

Mary went into the house to talk to Salem while Jesus went over to where the dye tanks were sitting. Each one contained a different color of dye. On the table were stacks of cloth which had been left by customers to be dyed.

Jesus took all the cloths, wrapped them together and placed them into the tank that held black dye. When Mary and Salem came out and saw what Jesus had done, he was very angry.

"Jesus, what have you done? All my work is for nothing. The cloths are ruined. What shall I do? You shall have to make this right. Mary, look! what your son has done. All my cloth is ruined. I am ruined."

Mary began to question Jesus, *"My beloved son, what hast thou done? Why have you done this? You should make me glad and not sad."*

Jesus answered: *"What did I do?"* *"See, you have destroyed all the work of this man."* Mary said,

Jesus said, *"How have I destroyed it?"* His mother answered, *"He had cloths from many people to dye each one a different color. You have made all of them one color, black. Now we must repair what you have done."*

Jesus asked the dyer what color he wanted
as he carefully took each cloth out of the dye.
Each cloth was dyed of the color desired.
He gave them unto the man.

The dyer and Mother Mary saw this.
Together, they glorified God and gave thanks.
They marveled at the miracle that was
wrought that day. Mary embraced Jesus and
with great relief and returned to her house.
Those who saw this miracle praised God.(22.7)

Water Stories

Several legends involving Jesus and his
mother have been given. As a baby, his bath
water contained a beautiful perfume which
when poured over a sick infant brought about
an instant healing. His clothes and blanket
likewise were filled with the healing energies
Jesus himself effused.

All water for household use had to be brought
from the well. It is said that Jesus was sent
by his mother to get water. He carried a jar-
type bucket common in that time. Not paying
attention to what he was doing, he dropped
the water jar. It broke.The water went all over
the ground. He quickly gathered the water up
into his mantle and carried it to his mother.
This indicates his powers over all the earthly
elements.(22.8)

Chapter 23

Later Nazareth Stories

"He shall be called a Nazarene." There is still in existence a Cordex Nazarethus, written in 1042 A.D. According to Pliny and Josephus, the Nazarene were a branch of the Essenes, often fair haired and light skinned who lived on the banks of the Jordan, 150 B.C.

Pythagoras is said to have been a pupil of an Assyria Nazareth, who was purported to have been the prophet Ezekiel. Nazarine (Nazars) from Arabic are Nabao and naba meaning "to wander" and to prophesy," The Essenes used only water in their rites; the Nazars used oil; Jesus used both. The Nazarene were a sect practicing severe asceticism and performing many miraculous healings. Their Initiations were called the "Mysteries of Life," In the ceremonials the candidate was put to death symbolicly, and through baptism resurrected into a new life.

Nazareth was not a place. Still today there is controversy as to its location. The Holy Family lived on the banks of the Jordan River, the trade route of many passing caravans from the East. Early in life Jesus would go out and converse with these travelers and gain knowledge concerning the Mysteries of the East. (23.1)

Jesus resembled his beautiful mother with fair skin and light auburn hair.Their intimate companionship was noticable. Jesus used much of the time during these quiet years to prepare Mary for her work as head of the Church in the days that were to follow the Resurrection. By means of a vision and the great wisdom of her son, she was made ready to assume the highest place ever given to a woman.(32.2)

In their many hours of daily communion with God, the Father, it was Jesus' wish that his mother remain with him. as the vessel and model of all perfection. (23.3)

Following the example of his mother, Jesus frequently visited the poor, ministered to the unfortunate, and healed the sick. The young Jesus spent many hours in travail trying to understand the transgressions of men and the Hebrew traditions he was being taught. He questioned Joseph frequently. Still, *his transmutative powers were such that the glory of heavens Light shone through him."(23.4)*

When they returned to Judea they lived in Galilee. He grew up in Nazareth of Galilee amidst the most spiritually advanced people in the world at that time, the dedicated Essenes. Like other Hebrew boys, he received his early education in his own home from his parents. Later he attended the synagogue school in Nazareth where the Scriptures were his first textbook.

The village of Nazareth was situated on a hillside in Galilee. Here one could live either an open or a secluded life. Looking from the hill above Nazareth to the west, which rose to the height of fifteen hundred feet above sea level, afforded an extremely broad view. To the west could be seen the Mediterranean, and Megido, commanding the great military roadway. To the south, Roman legions and camel trains in the plain of Esdraelon occupied the road. To the east, one could see Mt.Tabor and the cities of Decapolis teaming with Gentiles. Looking northward one saw the imposing view of Mt.Hermon with its snow-capped peak. In this panorama Jesus had constantly before him not only scenes of Hebrew history, but also the culture and aspirations of the larger Greco-Roman world.

Because of the busy trade route that passed here it is very possible that Jesus became proficient in several languages as claimed in some writings and the family had a thriving business. (23.5)

Joseph Builds Furniture

When Joseph went into the city to work, he

took Jesus with him. Whether he was
building gates, milk pails, sieves or boxes.
When he had anything that wasn't just right,
Jesus would stretch his hand towards it.
And it became perfect so Joseph had no need
to finish anything with his own hands, Being
of advanced age (approximately 96) he was
not very skillful at his carpenter's trade by
this time.

When Jesus was seven, the King of
Jerusalem sent for Joseph, and said, "I
commission thee to make me a comfortable
throne in which I sit to make the decisions for
Israel."

The throne was to be made of the same kind
of wood which was used in Solomon's time,
carved with various shapes and figures.(23.6)

Joseph began the work, which continued for
two years. He lived in the king's palace while
he was building the throne. When Joseph
came to fit the throne it was narrow by two
spans on each side of the appointed measure.
When the king saw it, he was very angry with
Joseph. Joseph was so afraid that
he could not eat supper. Finally, he sent word
for Jesus to come.

Jesus went to Joseph and asked him, "Why are
you so troubled?"

Joseph replied, *"I have lost my wages in the work which I have been about these two years. The throne is too small."*

Jesus said to him, *"Fear not. Take hold of one side of the throne, and I will take the other side. We will bring it to its correct dimensions."*

When Joseph had done as Jesus said, the throne obeyed, and was brought to its proper dimensions.

The king was delighted and paid Joseph handsomely.

Those who stood by saw the miracle were astonished, and praised God.

Joseph was also a farmer, as was almost every other man in Galilee at that time. He was skilled in making saddles and plows for his own use and his neighbors. If he was asked to make anything else it was quite rare. Furniture was unheard of in most homes.(23.7)

When Jesus was eight, Joseph was commissioned to build a bed for a rich man of the community. He went to gather the wood, and Jesus accompanied him. Joseph cut two trees and cleaned the branches off them with his ax. On setting together the boards, he discovered that one was too short. When he saw that, he was very discouraged and started to look for another.

Jesus said to him, "*Set the two boards together, even at one end.*"

Jesus motioned that Joseph should hold tight to the equal end of the beams while he pulled from the other end. Jesus said, "*Be at peace and do the work as you had planned.*" When Joseph saw that both beams were equal, He said, "*How blessed I am and thankful to God to have such a son.*"(23.8)

Sowing the Wheat

The sowing season came, and the child Jesus, went out with his father to sow their field with wheat. Jesus was given one small field to sow. While his father was sowing, the child Jesus sowed one measure of the grain in his field. It grew bountifully. When he harvested and threshed it, it yielded one hundred measures, far greater than the usual yield. He summoned all the poor in the village to the threshing floor and gave them all of his grain. Jesus was eight years old when he did this.(23.9)

Back to School

On three occasions Joseph attempted to put Jesus in school. A teacher, Zacchaeus overheard Jesus talking to Joseph one day called to Joseph *"You have a bright child with a good mind. Send him to my class and I will teach him to be mannerly."* Joseph said, *"No one has been able to discipline this boy. Perhaps God could. Don't think it will be easy"*.

Joseph took Jesus by the hand and led him into the classroom. The teacher wrote the alphabet for him and began the instruction by repeating the letter Alpha many times. But Jesus was silent and did not answer him.

Zacchaeus became angry and struck Jesus on the head. He took the blow calmly and said, *"I am the teacher. You are the student. I already know the letter you are teaching me. To you these letters are like a clashing cymbal which can't produce glory or wisdom because of the noise. Then he recited the letters from Alpha to Omega very quickly.*(8 p.373) (1 p.57) (Several similar stories from different sources.)

Then he told the teacher, *"You don't know the real nature of the letter, Alpha. How are you going to teach the letter Beta? "*

Jesus began to quiz Zacchaeus about the first letter, but he was unable to say any more.

Then, while many were listening, he said to Zacchaeus, *"Observe the design of the first letter: it has two straight lines proceeding to a point in the middle, gathered together, two cornered, not antagonistic, of the same family, proving the Alpha has lines of equal measure."*

Zacchaeus despaired of his teaching. He spoke to those who were present, *"Poor me. I'm utterly beside myself, wretch that I am. Why did I take this child: I have shamed myself. Take him away, I beg you, brother Joseph. I can't endure the lucidity of his speech. This child is not an ordinary mortal; perhaps he was born before the creation of the world...."* While those listening were advising Zacchaeus, Jesus laughed, *"Now let the infertile bear fruit and the blind see and the deaf in the understanding of their hearts, hear: I've come from above so that I might save those who are below and summon them to higher things, just as the one who sent me."*(23.9)

When the child stopped speaking, all those who had fallen under the curses he had made were instantly healed. (Some stories say he cast a curse on the teachers who tried to teach him.) And from then on no one dared to anger him for fear of being cursed and maimed for life.(23.10)

Playmate Falls Off the Roof Story

A few days later Jesus and his friends were playing on a housetop when one of the children leapt off the roof and died. The other children saw what had happened and ran away leaving Jesus standing there all by himself on the housetop.

The parents of the dead child accused Jesus. *"You are a troublemaker. You threw him down and now he's dead. You killed him."* Jesus responded, *"He threw himself down. He wasn't being careful and leapt down from the roof."*

Then Jesus leaped down from the roof and stood by the body of the dead child. In a loud voice he called *"Zeno! Get up and tell me: Did I push you?"*

Zeno got up immediately and said, *"No, Lord, you didn't push me. You raised me up."* Those who were present rejoiced and praised God.(23.12)

Healing of the Young Man's Foot

Later, nearby, a young man was splitting

wood when his ax slipped and cut off the bottom of his foot. It appeared he would die from the loss of blood.

A noisy crowd rushed to his side. Jesus ran to see what was happening. Forcing his way through the crowd, he grabbed hold of the young man's foot and it was instantly healed. He said to the youth, *"You can get up now and split your wood."* (23.13)

Snake Bite Story

Joseph sent his son James to tie up some wood and carry it back to the house, and Jesus followed his older step-brother. While James was gathering the firewood, a viper bit his hand. He lay sprawled out on the ground screaming with pain and dying. Jesus came and blew on the bite. The pain stopped, the snake burst apart, and James was healed.(23.14)

Later the same day, Jesus heard a woman wailing loudly after the death of her infant son. The neighbors were trying to console the poor woman. Jesus came quickly to see what the matter was.

He touched the baby's chest and said, *"I say to you, infant, you must live and be with your mother."* The infant looked up and laughed.

156

Jesus said to the woman, *"Take your baby to your breast, and remember me."*

Jesus went back to playing with the other children.(23.15)

Uniting With The Spirit Story

Mary told a story to Jesus, *"When you were young, before the Spirit came upon thee, you were in the vineyard one day helping Joseph tie up the vines and the Spirit came into my house. He looked exactly like you. I thought it was you."*

The Spirit asked, *"Where is my brother, Jesus? I want to meet with him."*

Mary continued, *"I was mystified. I thought it was a phantom talking to me. So, thinking I could detain him, I tied him up to the foot of the bed. Then I went to find you and bring you in to see what it was. I found Joseph staking up the vines and as I was telling him of the mystery, you arrived."*

When Jesus heard the news, he understood what was happening. He rejoiced, and the three hurried to the house. On coming to the house, *"Where is he? I must find him otherwise I will have to wait for him."* Jesus exclaimed,

Joseph was troubled when he heard Jesus say these words. Mary and Joseph entered the house together. They found the Spirit bound to the bed just as Mary had left him. They looked at the Spirit and then at Jesus. They looked exactly alike. Jesus untied the Spirit, and they embraced. When they kissed, they became one. (This is taken from Pistos Sofia, Gnostic, Third Century.)

Chapter 24

Lost in the Temple

Hebrew law required that every male go three times each year to Jerusalem and the women were required to go only once to the Feast of Passover, the time of the Spring Equinox.

At Bar Mitzvah, at the age of twelve the lad became the son of the Law and incurred his first legal obligation. A phylactery (broad band) inscribed with verses from the Bible was placed upon his brow as a reminder that he was to obey the word of God.

Though the Holy Family had risen above all outer law by becoming Essenes, they also obeyed all the old Temple customs. The Festival of the Passover continued for seven days, with different ceremonies on each day. On the third day it was lawful to return home.

When Jesus was twelve years old, Mary and Joseph brought Jesus to Passover for the first time. And thinking he was with friends when the feast was over, they returned (to Nazareth.)

In Jerusalem stood the magnificent Temple of marble and gold, built by Herod to placate the people for his many evil deeds.

Even as a youth, Jesus' insight into the wisdom of the ages he realized the difference between the letter of the law and its spirit. He had seen the worship of the nearby pagan temples, with their luxurious vices, sensuous music, and countless priests, and priestesses. In Jerusalem he saw the priests in their magnificent robes and costly jewels. The sacrifice of thousands of animals to atone for sins was repugnant to him. How far removed were these outward symbols of the worship of God from the holy radiant lives of Joseph and Mary and the other Essenes.(5 IV p.115)

But Jesus stayed behind in the Temple where there was an open forum among the doctors and elders and learned men of Israel. He asked several respectful but insightful questions and also gave answers. *"Whose son is the Messiah?"*

They answered, *"The son of David."*

"Why then, does he in the spirit call him Lord when he saith, The Lord said to my Lord, sit thou at my right hand, till I have made thine enemies thy footstool." Jesus questioned.

The principal Rabbi changed the subject and

asked him, " *Hast thou read books?* "

Jesus answered, that he had read both the
Scriptures, and the things which were
contained in books. And he was fluent in
many languages. He expounded to them from
the books of the law, and precepts, and
statutes, and the mysteries which are
contained in the books of the prophets;
keeping them questioning him for hours.
(24.2)

*"I never yet have seen or heard of such know-
ledge!   What do you think this boy will be?"*
questioned the Rabbi.

An astronomer, asked Jesus, whether he had
studied astronomy. Jesus explained the
number of the spheres and heavenly bodies,
as well as their triangular, square, and
sextile aspects; their progressive and
retrograde motion and their size. He gave
much information that had not yet been
discovered.

A philosopher, well skilled in physics and
natural philosophy, asked Jesus, if he had
studied physics.

Jesus explained to him physics and
metaphysics and also those things which
were above and below: Natural Law, the

power of nature, Physical Law, Mental Law and Spiritual Law and much about the physical body unknown to them...

The philosopher arose, and bowed down to Jesus, and said, *"O Lord Jesus, from henceforth I will be thy disciple and servant."*

While they were discoursing on these things, Mary and Joseph were passing in the hall and heard Jesus' voice. They came into the hall, having been three days walking about seeking Jesus.

When she saw him sitting among the elders, and in his turn proposing questions to them, and giving answers, Mary said, *"My son, why hast thou done thus to us? I and thy father have been at pains in seeking thee."*

He replied, *"Why did ye seek me? Did ye not know that I ought to be employed in my Father's house."* But they understood not the words which he said to them. Then the doctors of Law, Religion and Science asked Mary, *"Is this your son?"* And when she said, Yes, they said, *"O happy Mary, who hast born such a wise and learned son."*

Jesus returned with them to Nazareth and obeyed them in all things.

And his mother kept all these things in her mind; and Jesus grew in stature and wisdom, and favor with God and man.

From this time on, Jesus began to hide his studies, miracles and secret works. And he gave himself to the study of the law, till he arrived to the end of his thirtieth year. (24.2)

Another Source

On the day of Jesus' Bar Mitzvah, he with his two parents entered the Temple area. His mother departed from them to go into the women's gallery, Jesus objected to the separation. His visit to the area where animals were sacrificed also disturbed him. Instead of being filled with awe, he was filled with condemnation of the practices he witnessed.

Jesus, regarded still as a youth, was questioning the Priests and explaining the Law. The Priests were listening spellbound.

At the session on the second day Jesus had made bold to ask questions, and in a very amazing way he participated in the Temple discussion, but always in a manner consistent with his youth. He was respectful. On the third day with the scribes and teachers and others who came, spectators were also enjoying seeing a boy from Galilee confuse the wise men of the law. Some of his questions were recorded:

1. What really exists in the holy of hollies, behind the veil?
2. Why should mothers in Israel be segregated from the male Temple worshipers?
3. If God is a father who loves his children, why the slaughter of animals to gain divine favor--has the teaching of Moses been misunderstood?
4. Since the Temple is dedicated to worship of the Father in Heaven, is it proper to permit the presence of those who engage in barter and trade on Temple grounds?
5. Is the expected Messiah to become a temporal prince to sit on the throne of David, or is he to function as the light of life in the establishment of a Spiritual kingdom?

With the travail of his parents losing their son at the Temple and all that Jesus had heard and seen in that experience, filled him with agony.

Mary desired to console him by praying with him. As they knelt in prayer she saw a light from heaven overshadow Jesus and a voice saying: *"This is my beloved son in whom I am well pleased."* Both were restored to a peaceful attitude.

The Passover is a Jewish festival that celebrates Israel's liberation from Egyptian rule. All Jews were required to appear before the Lord at the Temple in Jerusalem at this time. Many people traveled together in pilgrimage. As the boy Jesus left the illustrious gathering of learned men, he took each one's hand and said, " I trust we shall meet again." (24.3)

A boy of twelve was regarded as a youth for yet two more years.This was very different for a girl who was considered ready for marriage.

Chapter 25

The Lost Years

Nazareth was one of twenty-four priest-led schools of the Hebrew nation. The Galilean center was notably more liberal in interpretation of the laws than the other schools. They were also more liberal regarding the observance of the Sabbath. Jesus attended the Synagogue school near his home. He was already a fluent reader, writer and speaker in Aramaic and Greek. The Nazareth Synagogue possessed a complete copy of the Scriptures in Hebrew and provided instruction in Hebrew only.

When Jesus was ten he graduated to the more advanced school where he committed to memory, by repetition, the deeper teachings of sacred law. At thirteen, he graduated and was turned over to his parents by the synagogue rulers as an educated "son of the commandment" and henceforth a responsible citizen of the commonwealth of Israel. He attended his first Passover that year with his father and mother.

Walking together on Sabbath afternoons was customary for Joseph and Jesus. They often climbed the highest hill near their home from which they could see all of Galilee. Northwest, on clear days, they could see the long ridge of Mount Carmel running down to the sea.

To the north, Mount Hermon raised its snowy peak in majestic splendor and monopolized the skyline, with its perpetual crown of snow. Far to the east they could discern the Jordan valley and far beyond lay the rocky hills of Moab.

To the south and east, they could see the Greco-Roman cities of Decapolis when the sun shone upon their marble walls, with their amphitheaters and pretentious Temples. In the west when they lingered til' sundown, they could make out the sailing vessels on the Mediterranean. From all four directions Jesus could watch camel caravan trains as they passed in and out of Nazareth.(25.1)

Many times Jesus heard his father relate the story of Elijah, one of the first of that long line of Hebrew prophets, who reproved Ahab and exposed the priests of Baal. (25.2)

Teaching the history of the Hebrew people to his son was Joseph's responsibility. It was on these frequent walks that Jesus developed his interest in nature.

Jesus' family was well known to the neighborhood and reference was made during Jesus' ministry regarding them. He was reported to have denied his families presence to teach the lesson to his students of who could become brethren in Christ. It was said that he did no healings in Nazareth, when he returned home. Urantia(25.3)

In addition to his formal schooling, Jesus began to make contact with the human nature of other peoples from the four corners of the known world and with the caravans from many lands as they passed in and out of his father's repair shop. It was a well-known way station with a spring nearby; rest and nourishment were available. Jesus learned to converse in Greek and other languages, with the travelers, and learned much about other peoples and the outside world.

Formal Schooling

On entering the local Synagogue school at seven (the law of compulsory education for boys had just been inaugurated) each boy was to choose his "birthday text," a rule to guide him throughout the years of study which would also be an important part of his graduation examination at thirteen. Jesus chose the passage from Isaiah: *"The spirit of the Lord God is upon me, for the Lord has*

*anointed me; he has sent me to bring good
news to the meek, to bind up the broken
hearted, to proclaim liberty to the captives, and
to set the spiritual prisoners free.* " (Isaiah 61:1)

The Synagogue also invited distinguished
visitors passing through the area on the
Sabbath to speak to the congregation, which
added to his education.

On Jesus' graduation, his teacher at the
Nazareth school commented to Joseph that
he feared "He had learned more from Jesus'
searching questions than he had been able
to teach him."(25.3)

Jesus entered as a student at Mt.Carmel
College after his bar mitzvah under the
name of Joshua Ben Joseph.The name Jesus
is synonymous with Joshua in the Hebrew
language. Jod is the most important letter in
their alphabet. It represents a part of each of
the twenty-two letters and signifies the power
of the ego, the I that will eventually become
the I Am.(25.4) At Mt. Carmel he studied with
the finest teachers and began to teach as
well.

The Families View of His Mission

From an early age Jesus realized that his
parents held quite different views regarding

169

his mission. He pondered over the matter. More and more he was inclined toward the view that Joseph held of the spiritual nature of his mission.

Mary was convinced during this time that her sons mission was political in nature and whenever possible turned the conversation to how he was to accomplish it. Jesus would gently touch her shoulder on these occasions and she would be silent. Saying *"My hour has not yet come."* And that ended the discussion.(25.5)

For several years,Jesus had been encouraged to read the scriptures in the local Synagogue; and when he turned fifteen he was invited to speak.

A visit from Elizabeth and John occurred in Jesus' eighteenth year. The two chosen young men agreed together that they would not meet again until baptism day at the Jordan river. Mentally they were in regular communication. (25.6)

Jesus' family suffered a great financial set-back and an emotional shock when Joseph died in a work accident. The family petitioned King Herod who had employed him for the past wages due and was refused. Jesus returned home to help support the family.

Joseph's Death

Joseph still had doubts on his death bed about Mary's virginity but he died peacefully in his bed at age 111. All of Joseph's children attended, Two of his sons were married by that time. It was said that Jesus was away traveling at the time of Joseph's death, but returned in out of body travel form to comfort his earthly father and support his mother.

Many Avatars of the past and some Apostles and Disciples have had the ability to make themselves visible to others at distant points. (25.7)

This account of Joseph's death is written as if Jesus were talking:
"I wept. My mother Mary asked if Joseph must die, and I told her that it must be. So, I sat at his head, Mary at his feet. I felt his heart and found that his soul was in his throat.

Mary felt his feet and legs and found them cold as death. The brethren and sisters were summoned. Lysia the eldest daughter (who is the seller of Purple dye) lamented: so did the whole family. I looked at the south door and saw Death, and Amente following with their satellites 'decani' armed with fire.

171

Joseph also saw them and was afraid. I rebuked them and they retreated. Death hid himself behind the door. I prayed the prayer for protection for the soul of Joseph 'until it crossed the seven aeons of darkness.' 'Let the river of fire be as water and the sea of demons cease vexing."

When I had said Amen, my mother spoke to me in the language of the inhabitants of the heavens,

Michael, Gabriel and the choir of Angels came. Numbness and panting seized on Joseph. Death, seeing me still present, dared not enter.

I arose and went outside to allow him to do his appointed work, but "deal gently," I cautioned.

Then Abaddon (Angel of destruction), went in and took the soul, Michael and Gabriel put the soul into a precious silken napkin, and the Angels took it away singing.

I (Jesus) sat down by the body and closed the eyes and mouth; and I spoke words that comforted Mary and the rest.

The people of Nazareth came and mourned til the ninth hour. Then I put all out of the house, washed and anointed the body. I prayed to my Father with the heavenly prayers which I

wrote with my own fingers on the tables of
Heaven before I took flesh in the holy Virgin
Mary.' Angels came and shrouded the body of
Joseph.

I blessed it from all corruption and pronounced
blessings on all who would celebrate his
memory by good deeds or write the story of
his death.

The chief men of the Temple came to prepare
the body, and found it already shrouded.

At the burial. I wept as the body was laid in
the tomb beside Jacob, his father." (25.8)

The story of Joseph's death contains many
mystical experiences that would not have
been understood by those of that time and/or
for many generations later.

Family Responsibilities

For a while after Joseph' death, Jesus
remained with his family gently teaching
them by wisdom and example, earning their
living in the saddle shop and also he became
proficient in metal working. Seeing that his
family was well supported by the other
children, Jesus went to Capernaum and
began fishing with his friends the Zebedee
family. Zebedee was a boat designer and

builder. He built fishing boats used on Lake Gallalee. Jesus began designing boats and designed a safer, more useful fishing boat for them. The funds from the sale of this popular boat were invested for him in a two-room house in Capernaum.(25.11)

As some of the children were married and seeing that the family was well situated financially, Jesus began distancing himself from them. His Mother was quite confused, and he spoke little to her about his plans. He sent money to assist the family from wherever he was, but he was often away for six months to a year or more at a time studying sometimes in other countries.

Jesus Travels

According to an account in the Talmud, Jesus studied in the temples of Egypt. Then he traveled to Persia where records of a young master, ascetic whom they called Issa, was ministering, teaching and healing the people. Ancient texts report that a young teacher came to India and later to China teaching the Fatherhood of God and the Brotherhood of Man who also protested the emptyness of ceremonial worship. (25.12) According to Urantia teaching, Jesus, in his twenty-ninth year, became the tutor of a wealthy Egyptian boy whose father was a traveling business man. The father was welcomed by heads of state through out the known world as his goods were rare and of the highest quality. Jesus may have traveled for a year or more with Gonod and his son, Ganid, to the various capitols of the known world as the youth's tutor. He was welcomed as an interpreter in many courts where Gonod had business. During this time his family and Mary did not know where he was but, believed he was at the great library and school in Alexandria, studying and teaching as he had been asked to do several years prior. He did visit there and spent much of that time in the study of various religions.

As a translator-tutor Jesus was of great service to Gonod and by the courts he visited. Though the businessman entreated Jesus to return to India with him, guaranteeing that his teaching would be especially welcome in that land, he refused. *"My time is not come to minister to my people. My responsibility is to my family,"*(25 13)

Jesus and John's Friendship

Jesus and John always experienced a soul tie and were close because they were born into the same family. They grew together in strength and wisdom. They were known to have communicated regularly on the higher

175

planes. When Jesus presented himself for baptism by his cousin John, they both knew it was preordained.

John being fatherless at a very young age and his mother of advanced years, he asked permission of his mother to live with a holy man of the desert to prepare for his mission. His companionship with his parents continued in spite of their demise from this physical plane. Legends say that John was blessed with a beautiful childhood and that he was frequently illumined in his words and being. He grew in wisdom and stature with God, as did his cousin, Jesus. John was so sheltered in the desert as a youth that he found it difficult to adjust to city life as an adult. (25.14)

Meanwhile, John the Baptist tended his sheep and was eagerly awaiting his time to come forward. He made a lifetime vow and had joined the Nazarite sect. Much of his time was spent reading from their manuscripts at Engedi.

Though a son of a Priest of the Temple, John came from the wilderness of Judea dressed in a camels hair cloak, with a leather girdle about his loins, living on locusts and honey. His coming was prophesied by Esias saying,

*"The voice of one crying in the wilderness.
Prepare the way of the Lord, make his paths
straight."* (25.15)
He went about baptizing and calling for the
people to repent though he claimed to only be
able to baptize with water and the one to
come would baptize with the Holy Ghost and
with fire.

To most of the Hebrew people the promise of
the kingdom of heaven on earth meant that
the throne of King David would again be
filled, and they would be free from the Roman
yoke. John realized that he was the
messenger to usher in this time of change.
Elijah was the example he followed. He was
well educated in the sacred writings and an
eloquent, powerful speaker.
(25.16)

Mary and Jesus were frequently with him in
spirit through out his life. They visited him
when he was imprisoned by Herod Antipas.
Hosts of Angels attended him and his cell was
filled with light. Mary and Jesus were with
him in spirit when his time of martyrdom at
the hands of Herod came. He gave his life
willingly as he had completed his task of
being the first martyr for the Christ.(25.17)

Chapter 26

Beginning of the Ministry

The Baptism

Jesus was baptized at the very height of
John's preaching when Palestine was aflame
with the expectancy of his message--"*the
kingdom of God is at hand*"--when all Jewry
was engaged in serious and solemn self-
examination. The Jewish sense of racial
solidarity was profound. They not only
believed that the sins of the father might
afflict his children, but they firmly believed
that the sin of one individual might curse the
nation. Not all who submitted to John's
baptism regarded themselves as guilty of the
specific sins which John denounced. Many
devout Jews were baptized by John for the
good of Israel. They feared lest some sin of
ignorance on their part might delay the
coming of the Messiah... In accepting baptism
at the hands of John, Jesus was following
the example of many pious Israelites. *(26.1)*

On a visit with his family in Nazareth Mary
said to Jesus, *"John the Baptist is baptizing
for the forgiveness of sins. Let's go down to
Pella and get baptized by him."*

Jesus answered, *"But how have I sinned? Why*

*should I go and be baptized by him? Only if I
don't know what I'm talking about."*

The purpose of this passage by Jerome (early
writings of the Holy family) was purported to
indicate that Jesus was not having the
baptism for forgiveness of his sins but to
indicate that his family, including the Mother
Mary, also participated.

The mystic experience of the Baptism, is a
spiritual awakening of the Initiate,
acknowledged by a spiritual matching from
above; the state of Grace is achieved. The
dove of spiritual power, parts the clouds of
human consciousness and the voice of God is
heard saying: *"Thou art my beloved in whom I
am well pleased."* (26.2)

John the Baptist was baptizing at Pella on
the Jordan river. The sons of Zebedee, the
fisherman and boat builder, had been
baptized by John and they listened to him preach
on weekends. Jesus was working in the boat-
building business for Zebedee and had
designed a unique new fishing boat that
became popular, which resulted in Zebedee
becoming very wealthy.

Jesus received word that his family, James,
Jude and others, perhaps his mother were
coming to see him and wanted to go on to the

Jordan River to be baptized by John. The night before their arrival Jesus spent the entire night in prayer. The next day when his family arrived, he put away his tools, removed his work apron and said to the other workman, *"My hour has come. Let us go to John at Pella."*

When they arrived at the river John had just begun to baptize for that day. The line of believers awaiting baptism was long. John had heard of Jesus' favorable remarks regarding his preaching and was hoping to see him. He was surprised to find Jesus waiting in the line. He stopped the baptisms and asked,

"Why do you come to me? I should be coming to you for baptism."

" I must set an example for my family and those others who know that my time has come. Jesus replied.

When Jesus went down to the River Jordan to be baptized, he was a mortal of the realm who had attained the pinnacle of human evolutionary ascension in all matters related to the conquest of the mind and to self-identification with the Spirit. He stood in the Jordan that day a perfected mortal of the evolutionary worlds of time and space. Perfectly

*synchronized and with full communication
between the mortal mind of Jesus and the
indwelling spirit Adjuster, the divine gift
of his Father in Paradise. (26.3)*

*John was noticeably trembling as he prepared
to baptize Jesus of Nazareth at noon on
January 14, A.D. 26. When Jesus stepped
down into the River Jordan to be baptized,
great balls of fire appeared on the surface of
the water, and he heard the words of the
sacred rite, "This is my beloved Son, in whom I
am well pleased." And he shone with a great
white light. (26.4)*

On coming out of the water the Holy Spirit, in
the form of a dove flew overhead saying, "*My
son, I was waiting for you in all the prophets,
waiting for you to come so I could rest in you.
For you are my rest; you are my first begotten
Son who rules forever.*" (26.5)

A great change came over the countenance of
Jesus. The river boiled, the rocks groaned
and the white dove circled overhead. John
told the story that he had heard from his
mother, Elizabeth regarding their births.

The Baptism of the Blessed Mary

The first work of the Lord Christ after his
Baptism was the endowing of the blessed lady

with the three fold powers of the Trinity. The early Church legends beautifully describe this high ceremonial as Mary, surrounded by host of chanting Angels, is baptized. Jesus bestowing upon her the powers of will, wisdom and the Volition Principles of Spirit. The Father or Will Principle intones: *"This is my beloved Daughter in whom I delight.* The word or Christ declares: *This is my beloved Mother who will assist me in all my works.* The Holy Ghost who blends and unites the two before mentioned adds: *"This is my Bride chosen from among thousands." (26.6)*

Jesus walked silently out into the desert and was not seen again for forty days and nights.

Jesus' brothers were baptized also.(26.5)

From this time on it was clear to John the Baptist that Jesus was the Messiah: *"Now I know of a certainty that Jesus is the Deliverer.* "His preaching became more pointed and fervent causing much attention from the Pharisees. (26.7)

Origen, (a later writer,) revealed that, Jesus said, *" Just now The Holy Spirit, my mother, took me by one of my hairs and brought me to Tabor, the great mountain." (26.8)*

After the Baptism and the forty days in the

wilderness, Jesus and his mother moved to his house in Capernum. There Jesus' ministry expanded. Mary's work was concentrated upon healing children and teaching their mothers. When the day's work was done, Jesus and his Mother would often spend the night in prayer in the hills under the stars, or beside the Lake of Galilee. (26.9)

Wedding at Canna, Galilee

Mary and family were invited to a wedding in Cana, Galilee, which was a three day journey north of Nazareth. Jesus was also invited to bring his Disciples. Weddings were often a three-day affair which was quite an expense for the families. After two days the wine ran out. Mary said to Jesus, "They're out of wine."

Jesus replied to her, " Woman, It is not my time yet."

His mother said to the servants, "Whatever he tells you, do it."

At the entrance of the house there were six large, stone water jars for use in the Jewish rite of purification. Each could hold twenty to thirty gallons.

"Fill the jars with water," Jesus ordered the servants. So they filled them to the brim. "Now

dip out some wine and take it to the Wedding Master."

When the Wedding Master tasted the water, now changed into wine, he had no idea from where it had come. He called the groom and said to him, "Everyone serves the good wine first and only later, when people are drunk, the cheaper wine. But you've held back the best wine until now."(26.10)

Mary was dancing with glee within herself. She did not know how the wine would be produced, but she confidently believed that she had finally persuaded her son to assert his authority, to dare to step forth and claim his position and exhibit his Messianic power...She was not disappointed... The wine Mary desired...was forthcoming. (26.11)

Jesus performed this first miracle in Cana, Galilee. It displayed his mastery over the elements of the material world, and his disciples believed in him.

Then they went down to Capernaum, but they stayed there only a few days.

Later in Jesus' ministry he had become a wanted man, and it was often difficult as Mary, the family, and many of the Disciples were being watched. He stopped going home for that reason. Those who did get through the maize of scrutiny set up by the faithful often had to explain themselves and/or present themselves as true believers.

Some accounts say that there was fear, distrust and hard feelings between Jesus and his family. Certainly, there was confusion as to his mission. The fragments that we have may give a misleading view of their family attitudes.

Mother Mary's Visit Mentioned

And there came to him his mother and his brothers, and they were not able to speak to him because of the crowd.

And they said to him, Your mother and your brothers are standing outside, and they want to see you.

He answered, saying to them, "These are my mother and my brothers, those who hear the word of God, and do it.
(26.12)

Mary remained steadfast in her support of her sons mission on earth. Though they could not communicate in person, they continued to spend much time in spiritual communion. Jesus' half-brothers were supportive, but not as yet convinced of his Divine calling.

Early in his ministry Jesus had cast the money changers out of the Temple which caught the attention of the Romans and the priests; he became a wanted man.

Jesus also was releasing his earthly ties to family.

The Transfiguration

And after six days Jesus taketh with him Peter, and James, and John, his brother and bringeth them up in to a high mountain apart, And was transfigured before them: and his face did shine as the sun, and his raiment was white as the light. And, behold, there appeared unto them Moses and Elias talking with him.

Then answered Peter, and said unto Jesus, "Lord it is good for us to be here: if thou wilt, let us make here three tabernacles; one for thee, one for Moses, and one for Elias."

While he yet spake, behold, a bright cloud overshadowed them: and behold a voice out of the cloud, which said, "This is my beloved Son, in whom I am well pleased; hear ye him."

And when the Disciples heard it, they fell on

their faces, and were sore afraid.

And Jesus came and touched them, and said, "Arise, and be not afraid."

And when they had lifted up their eyes, they saw no man, save Jesus only. (26.12)

The Mystery Described

The true meaning of the Transfiguration was defined in these esoteric writings:

When the candidate reaches a place of holiness, equal balance between the opposite polarities have been established. With this step comes the full flowering of the two spiritual organs in the head, the pituitary and the pineal glands. These two lighted organs are now lighted lamps of the body temple. The pineal gland crowns the masculine or fire column, named the column of Joseph, and the pituitary gland crowns the feminine or water column, named the column of Mary. As the light emanating from these two glands unites through the third ventricle of the brain which lies between the two, this point in the head is transformed into a veritable manger of light and the focal point for the activity of the Christ principle in the life of the candidate. The earliest manifestation of this principle occurred at the Degree of the Holy birth... The expanding

*light which extends beyond the periphery of the
head forms the radiant halo of the saints.
Gradually this halo is extended until it
envelops the entire body in what is described
as the golden wedding garment. The creation of
this luminous soul body is a requisite for
entrance into the still higher Degrees of the
Mysteries. (26.13)*

Jesus and Mary were well aware of the
outcome of his ministry. He prophesied
frequently about his death. Mary was rarely
mentioned during Jesus' ministry. Her job at
that time was to sustain and counsel the
women who followed Jesus, which she did
very well.

The Passover Week

*Six nights before the feast of Passover Jesus
and Mother Mary returned to Betheny, a few
miles from Jerusalem to the home of their most
spiritually advanced followers: Lazarus and
his two sisters, Martha and Mary. Lazarus
(meaning God assists) was the one Jesus had
raised from the dead after being in the tomb for
four days, a while before. Lazarus understood
the Mysteries and the higher purpose his
death would serve. When Jesus summoned him
from the grave, he responded and came forth
having completed his Initiation.
Jesus spent each night instructing these*

Apostles in the Higher Mysteries. It is interesting to note that two of these were women at a time when women were not respected.

The true significance of Mary's breaking the alabaster vase at the Master's feet and anointing them with fragrant oil indicates   that she stood upon the threshold of the Temple of Light, the Second Degree.

Martha was not as yet ready for the spiritual promotion. Lazarus, however, sat at the table with the Master.

On Tuesday the Master gave the disciples both men and women advanced work leading up to the Resurection Rite.

Wednesday, Judas surccumbed to the temptation of the high priests which indicated he had not succeeded in passing the First Degree, or Rite of Purification.(27.1)

Chapter 27

It Is Accomplished

The Triumphal Entry

The scene of the Triumphal Entry was
Jerusalem, the City of Peace, representing the
heart or love center of the body wherin the
Christ spirit first comes to life. The palms
strewn on His path represent victorious
attainment. The young donkey on which Jesus
rode symbolizes the Ancient Wisdom. Jesus
had sent Peter and John to find the colt and
bring it to him. That the disciples were able to
bring back the colt signified that they had
become Initiates of the Christian Mysteries.

Mary, Mary Magdalene, Mary of Cleophis and
Veronica were the only women mentioned.
Many other women disciples were among the
throngs who lined the sacred way into
Jerusalem chanting hosannas and singing
praises, waving palm branches and scattering
flowers as Jesus came riding a donkey colt into
Jerusalem. They witnessed the overwhelming
adulation of the faithful that encircled their
precious teacher. Some realized the deeper
meaning that outlined the Path of Initiation that
concluded the earthly work of the Master.

Every event in the life of Jesus during the

Passion time represents some phase of Initiation into the Christian Mysteries. For the Initiates the Triumphal Entry signifies the joys of the Path and Calvary symbolizes the sorrows.

The Angelic chorus joined in the singing of "Peace on Earth, good will toward men" (27.1)

The Passover

Then the day of unleavened bread came, on which it was the custom to kill the passover lamb. So Jesus sent Peter and John, and said, Go and prepare us the passover for us to eat. They said to him, "Where do you wish us to prepare?"

He said to them, "Behold, when you enter the city, you will meet a man carrying a water skin; follow him wherever he enters,"

Say to the master of the house, "Our Teacher asks, Where is the guest room, where I may eat the passover with my disciples?"

And behold, he shall shew you an upper room, large and furnished; there make ready.

And they went, and found it just as he had said to them; and they prepared the passover feast.

And when it was time, Jesus came and sat down, and the twelve Apostles with him.

And he said unto them, I have greatly desired to eat this passover with you before I suffer; (27.2)

In the Upper Room the feast was held where the Master taught the higher mysteries. Traditionally women did not attend any meeting and would not be mentioned as that was not acceptable. The Mother Mary and many other women Disciples were present (according to the escoteric writings) keeping in perfect balance the masculine and feminine principles that the Master taught and demonstrated. (27.3)

The Way of the Cross

The Blessed Mary was not present at the Garden of Gethsemane, but she was completely in tune and supportive of her son as he began his difficult journey to Christhood. She supported him equally in joy and grief.

Mother Mary, Mary Magdalene, Mary of Cleophas and Veronica and many other women disciples mingled with the turbulent crowd on the way to Golgotha. And Veronica offered her handkerchief to wipe away the blood on the Master's brow. The women held the vigil while many of the male disciples hid themselves or denied the Master, but the women bravely did not. The Master blessed and strengthened them with his love.

Mary stayed with her son, the Avatar, the Christos until his body was taken down from the cross and put into her waiting arms. Mary was faithful to the end. She became the most advanced of all the Disciples and was made the leader and teacher of them all.(27.4)

John's Promise

Now there stood by the cross of Jesus his mother, and his mother's sister, Mary, the wife of Cleophas, and Mary Magdalene.

When Jesus therefore saw his mother, and the disciple standing by, whom he loved, he saith unto his mother; "Woman, behold thy son!" Then saith he to the disciple, "Behold thy mother!" And from that hour that disciple took her unto his own home. (27.5) The Master Jesus might possibly have given her care into a male relative had one been there.Later, she did live in Jerusalem and serve the early Church through James the Just, her stepson.

Last Words of Jesus

The last words of Jesus were said to be,
" *My God, My God, Why has thou forsaken me?*
It is finished." (27.6)
Another translation from NCV, a foot note are
"Father, Father, How thou hast glofied me. For
this was I born. This is my destiny. It is
accomplished."

And when Jesus had cried with a loud voice,
he said, *"Father, unto thy hands I commend my*
spirit:" and having said this, he gave up the
ghost. (27.7)

Then Jesus, the Christ was taken down from
the cross and given to his mothers waiting
arms. Quickly the body was taken to a tomb
of Joseph of Arimathea before sunset to
prevent the defiling of the Jewish Day of
Preparation.(27.8)

This Avatar, Jesus, already knew from birth
who he was, the Lord of Urantia,(Earth) and
why he was here, to point the way for
humanites upliftment. He took residence in
human form to aid human kind in their
evolution from God to God and to show that
death is not final and that life is eternal. He
returned in recognizable form several times
and can return any time he choses.

All humans have this same ability as Jesus said, "...*the works that I do shall he do also, and greater works than these, shall ye do*;" (27.9)

Chapter 28

Mary's Initiation at the Foot of the Cross

Mary had prepared for a long time to take over the leadership of the esoteric Christian work following the Resurrection of her son. Because of her high level of consciousness she was acclaimed the leader of the early Christian Church until her Ascension. Of course, a woman could not achieve such status so her stepson James was given that honor.

It is said that the Mother Mary spent many hours alone at the foot of the cross. There she passed and mastered the Third Degree.

She revealed her initiation at the foot of the cross. "An astounding mystery my beloved one revealed to me at Golgotha. A shining cloud came and took me up to the Third Heaven and set me down at the boundary of the earth. I looked out and saw that the whole world was like nothing. I was invited to review the Akashic Records, the Cosmic Scrolls standing before me as a endless pillar of gold covered over with inscriptions."

She described the examination of an incoming soul. The soul lamented, "I did not know all this would take place. Had I known I would never have given sleep to my eyes. I would never have eaten food or drunk water until I had obtained a little rest from the Father, the Son and the Holy Ghost."

"The soul was examined by three Spirits: the Spirit of Fornication, the Spirit of Pride, and the Spirit of Falsehood. Each one found evidence of their portion residing therein."O Soul, thou art not yet ready to enter Heaven. Thou hast loved the darkness greater than the light."(28.1)

Mary also witnessed the liberation of a righteous soul. " saw shining Angels and in their hands were a golden sensor in which incense was burned. They surrounded him, crowned him with light and said,
" Come forth, thou soul of peace! Rejoice, O pure bright soul and be glad. I participated with the Angels to salute him and sang words of joy with them. The Father gave to that soul a white garment, whiter than milk, and three shining crowns brighter than the Sun and Moon. And God called the Archangel Michael and said unto him: "Take this soul to the Garden of Delight."

She proceeded to the First Heaven where she met many of the prophets including Elizabeth and John the Baptist. She related that she saw a city which was shining more brightly than the Sun or Moon with many flowers and fruits.

The Second Heaven was a white land that shone seven times more brightly than the Sun, Moon and Stars, decorated with gold and silver.

She was carried to the Third Heaven in a ship of gold. There the white houses gleamed with couches of gold. Many came to great her who had overcome the world, wearing their jeweled crowns.

In the heavenly Jerusalem, home world of the Christ and where John received inspiration for his Revelation, she saw a sanctuary of light, a pavilion of light and a tent covered with fire and was greeted by David who sang praises in her honor accompanied on his harp which caused the garden to shake with its intensity.

Her next ascent was to the city of God, the Divine Spirit, where she saw a shining city built in the form of a rose. She was told that this exalted sphere is available to those who have attained the Christ consciousness and have developed the androgynous power of the Holy Ghost.

The Virgin Mary's life experience was in preparation for her translation into the angelic kingdom. Jesus the Christ, granted her a throne in the city of Angeles where she has thousands of Angels to perform her important work with women and children. (28.2)

Mary was "filled with the powers of the Holy Ghost." This high Initiate was known as Mary of Bethlehem and often referred to in the esoteric Wisdom of the early Church as the "Bride of the Holy Ghost."

The esoteric view is that, *All life evolving on the planet Earth is under the guidance of the Third Aspect of the Godhead (Holy Ghost). Its force is considered positive and negative, masculine and feminine, will and imagination, intellect and love.*

Mary was guided by the attention of the Holy Ghost as she was the supreme Initiate of all earthly women, had perfected the image-building, feminine faculty of Spirit. (28.3)

The Purpose of the Christian Mysteries

The purpose of the Christian Mysteries (from which most of this material is taken) is to develop purity, love and faith in preparation to guide one along the path of strength, firmness of purpose and dedication. Service to our fellow man is stressed as soul building.

The purpose of the these Mysteries is to initiate the believer into a state of immortality, and to gain freedom from the limitation of the physician body.

Selflessness, purity and dedication mark the Rite of Gethsemane. When developed in the Initiate, one is prepared for that rite.

The rite of Transmutation parallels Jesus' agony on the cross and assists one in raising the vibratory rate to the celestial state and frees one's spirit to become interplanetary. The vision occurring as this state is reached is as a kaleidoscopic view of the original purpose seared by the energies of the earthly view. This is represented in the Master's words, " Let this cup pass from me, nevertheless not as I will...Thus laying down the physical body means the transmutation of its elements into Spirit, hence it becomes invisible to mortal eyes."(28.4)

Lessons of the Initiates

Plato says: "Each pleasure and pain is a sort of nail which rivets soul to body. " The spirit is cognizant to the five senses. The five nails that rivet the soul to body must be cleansed by the spirit fire. This fire ignites the pineal and pituitary glands in the head and the crown of thorns becomes the halo of light. The scarlet robe becomes the royal purple.

Those victorious ones who follow the pathway of the Christian Mysteries discover great liberation between the physical plane and the

Spiritual Realms. In so doing, the soul joins the multitude of voices raised in saluting God, as the Master Jesus did in his last words, "My God, my God, how hast thou glorified me." (28.5)

The Way of the Cross

Only three persons were advanced enough to follow the Master through the stations of the Cross. The Divine Mother Mary, John the beloved, and Mary Magdalene were sufficiently evolved to make the journey.

As a result Mother Mary accompanied her son into the inner worlds and was revealed to her again the planetary mission and the plan that was being carried out.

Many translations of the last words of Jesus the Christ exist. He did not sorrow over being forsaken, rather he exalted by his elevation. "My Father, how thou hast glorified me!" he said as he passed his final test to the Christhood. This is the path to Glory.

On the higher level it is known that Jesus the Christ appeared first to his Mother Mary. So sublime was the divine rapture of this meeting of soul to soul that no earthly record was made of it.

Mary of Magdalene entered the Third Degree when she met the Master in the Garden. At first she did not recognize him resplendent in his spiritual body. He gradually assisted her to lift her consciousness to his level where she then knew him and sank to her knees in humbleness and addressed him as "Rabboni," meaning most high Master.(28.6)

At the Rite of Pentecost the Mother Mary and the twelve disciples were given healing powers through the use of love and light. (28.7)

From the writing of Bartholomew comes this vignette: The Father sent the Son down into Galilee to console the apostles and Mary: and he came and blessed them and showed them his wounds, and committed them to the care of Peter, and gave them their commission to preach. They kissed his side and sealed themselves with the blood that flowed thence. Then he went up to heaven. (28.8)

The Initiate is lifted above the level of humanity as the descent of the power of the Holy Ghost endows one with greater power and makes one a citizen of the Angelic Kingdom. An exalted soul of this level works with Angels as his brothers, such was Mary's attainment and also was the attainment of the Disciples after Pentecost.

Mary was the acknowledge leader of the esoteric Christian community after the ascension of the Christ in secret, despite the fact that in the outer world not she, but John, Peter or James were preeminent. Womens status in the world at that time was very low and they could not speak out in public or travel about with safety. (28.9))

Her mission was not over. She continued to lead the disciples, and through her efforts many who were doubting stayed true to their paths as she became their advisor and confidante. ...Mary's spiritual authority was accepted without question in the community of Christians.

Mary was always accompanied by a group of devoted women who witnessed by night and by day the miracles she performed. Mary was considered to be a 'glorious woman'. (28.10)

Mary Speaks of the Immaculate Conception

During the time after the crucifixion when the apostles came together, the disciple Bartholomew came close to Mary and with a cheerful countenance he ask her how it was that she was able to conceive the incomprehensible and bring forth such greatness.

At first she refused the request saying that she would be prevented from speaking about it, Finally, after the apostles pressed the question, she agreed.

She began with a prayer mainly describing the power of the Godhead. In her closing she requested permission to reveal how it came to be. Then she requested that they all sit down on the ground and with Peter, Andrew, John and Bartholomew supporting her body she began her story.

I was praying in the Temple when The Holy Spirit said to me, "Hail, thou that are highly favored, the chosen vessel, grace inexhaustible." And he brought forth a loaf of bread and a glass of wine. After he had eaten and drunk his fill he gave some to me to eat, but the loaf was untouched and the cup of wine full.

Then he said to me: "In three years I will send my word unto thee and thou shalt conceive my son and through him shall the whole creation be saved. Peace be unto thee, my beloved. My peace shall be with thee."

Then he vanished from my sight.

As she was saying this, fire issued out of her mouth and Jesus appeared and laid his hand upon her mouth and the flame ceased. (28.11)

Chapter 29

Time to Leave

The type pattern of the New Age (Aquarian Age) in the matter of prenatal preparation was brought to earth by the Initiate Mary of Bethlehem and she also gave the type-pattern for the translation from earth to heaven in the divine adventure of death. She demonstrated for all human kind the New Age realization that death is a Translation, not a rupture of consciousness, but fittingly termed "Spirit in action."(29.1)

It was Mary's daily practice to go to Jesus' tomb to pray. Some Pharisees continued to threaten her life and reported her visits to the Governor. He ordered her to stay away. But, she did not. They would wait for her, then verbally abuse her and threaten to stone her. The second time they went to the Governor regarding Mary, he told them to manage the matter themselves.

It was said that the Governor took his sick son to Mary and she healed him.

The Mother Mary attended a festival along with a group of her women followers. She was recognized by a mother whose child she had healed. Mother after mother came to her for healing; then others came, and eventually she had healed 2,800 persons.(29.2)

The Angry Jews

A group of Pharisees were intent on ridding Israel of this Christian cult lead by Jesus. After he was crucified they turned their anger on the Mother Mary. At least three accounts in the ancient literature are recorded of their verbal assault on her. Word came to her again that the Pharisees were coming, and she was taken the twelve miles to Bethlehem for safety.

When the crowd found the place empty, they were even more angry. They tried to set the house on fire where they thought she had been and set themselves on fire instead. (29.3)

Mary's Translation

Mary realized that her stay on earth was very dangerous, she longed to be with her son and she prayed to be released from this life,

One day Mary was praying beside the Holy Tomb when the heavens opened and the Angel Gabriel appeared to her and said: *"Thou art to go forth soon from this fleeting world into the life which is forever."*

Mary immediately called the Virgins, her attendants, and said,*"I am going to Bethlehem, if there be any among you who desire to come with me, let her do so..."* They replied as one voice:, *"We will all go with you. We will not separate from you all the days of our life."*

As Mary was preparing to go to Bethlehem there came an Angel dressed in golden robes of great brightness came before her, greeting her: *"Hail, thou blessed of the Lord, I bring you greetings from your beloved son, Jesus. Your prayers have been answered. I present to you this palm branch from the garden of the Unnameable. You will cause it to lead the way in front of your bier."* And he gave her the palm branch all bright and shiny. *" You will be taken up out of the body on the third day. Thy son, the Angels and all powers of heaven await thy coming."*

Then Mother Mary asked that the Apostles of the Lord Jesus Christ be gathered to her. And the Angel said, *"By the power of my Lord Jesus Christ all the Apostles will be brought from far and near, and also from the tomb, to be with you."*

The Disciples had scattered throughout the known world after the descent of the Holy Ghost at Pentecost, proclaiming the glad tidings. As their spiritual attainment transcended the limitations of time and space, they often traveled in their spiritual vehicles to meet Mary at her sanctuary in Bethlehem.

Mary knew that they had been transported frequently in night journeys of the soul described as "borne in a shining cloud," or "riding in a chariot of light." or upon the "wings of a great bird," These are mystical descriptions of soul flights. The Disciples were clothed in the radiance of their celestial bodies...They instantly responded to the spirit-call of Mary.

This was also true for those who had left this plain putting aside their physical bodies in so-called death as those who still remained in earthly embodiment. Death is just an interlude to the Initiates of this exalted degree as the time between waking and sleeping, between the outer and the inner, between heaven and earth. It was for this reason that the Disciples came to imbibe further wisdom from the blessed Mary in Bethlehem. It was for this reason also that she chose this sacred place, Bethlehem for this sublime ceremonial of the Mystical Death. (29.4)

The Mystical Death

Mary had a request of the Angel, *"I ask that the powers of hell will not touch my soul and I will not see the prince of darkness. Please bless me."* The Angel said, *"The powers of hell shall not hurt thee and the Lord thy God has blessed you. I am just the messenger of the Lord. I cannot grant any favors. The favors you ask can only be granted by him whom you carried in your womb, for he is all power, world without end."* the Angel departed(29.5)

The palm branch shone with exceeding brightness in her darkened room, and the Mother Mary remembered whence it came: that hot day on the journey to Egypt that they were hungry and sore with thirst. The palm bent down to her feet and all ate their fill of its fruit. The palm also gave up the water from beneath its roots and saved man and beasts from thirst.

Taking off her garments Mary bathed herself. She put on her best garments. Taking the shining palm, she went to pray. And having comforted her soul, she returned to her dwelling.(29.6)

John was preaching at Ephesus on the Lord's day at the third hour when an earthquake came, and he was raised up in a

cloud that took him out of sight. He was told
to come to see Mary before she goeth out of
the world. He found himself the first to arrive
before the door in Bethlehem where Mother
Mary was.

Mary rejoiced when she saw John who had
been given charge of her by her son Jesus on
the cross. She told him that in three days she
was to leave her body. (29.7)

She took John into her bed chamber and
showed him her grave clothes and the palm
of light. She asked him to carry it before the
bier as she was being taken to her tomb.

John protested, *"How shall I do this all alone?
All the Apostles must come to honor thee."*

On cloud after cloud the Apostles began to
arrive from their ministries. Some had loosed
their grave cloths and came from their tombs.
There were John, James his brother, Peter,
Paul, Andrew, Philip, Luke, Barnabas,
Bartholomew, Matthew, Matthias surnamed
Justus, Dimon the Canaanite, Jude and his
brother Nicodemus, Maximianus (this must
be the legendary Maximin of Aix-en-Provence
coming from Mary Magdalene's mission to
Marseilles) and James the half brother of
Jesus. Thomas was absent. (29.8)

The followers of the Lord greeted each other with great joy and marveled at the miracle, asking each other *"Why are we here?"* And Paul who was taken from a circumcision ministering with Barnabas to the Gentiles marveled at why this gathering together.

A slight contention arose among them on who was the most worthy to pray asking the Lord Jesus why they were brought to this place in Bethlehem. Peter suggested that Paul do the prayer. Paul declined turning the idea back to Peter saying, *"Thou wast chosen of God to be a pillar of the church, and are before all in apostleship."* So Peter prayed and John appeared coming from the house and they went in and found Mary awaiting them.

Mary saluted them saying, *"Blessed be thou beloved of the Lord which made heaven and earth. Peace be unto you my most beloved brethren. How came you hither?"*

They each told her the circumstance of their coming from far and near, each one having been lifted up into a cloud by the Spirit and set down at her door.

Mother Mary revealed the reason for their coming, and asked them to attend and pray with her until her transition, which was to take place in three days. And all the Disciples stayed with her and blessed her. As they talked, they reminded Mary of her: steadfast loyalty, her wisdom, and support of the Disciples, her leadership of the women, her understanding of the Master's purpose, her gentle nature and her continued gift of love to all.

Many faithful women were accompanying Mary: Calietha, daughter of Nicodemus, Neshra, daughter of Gamaliel, Tabitha, daughter of Archelaus. And many others attended Mary: Hanna, Mary's mother and Elizabeth her cousin, including the seven Temple virgins were present.(29.9)

The Assumption

On that Sunday at the third hour, it is said that the time of harvesting had come for Mary, the Mother of Jesus.

At the appointed hour, Mary's Translation took place in cosmic splendor. The Heavens shook, the doors of the firmament were open wide, the Earth reeled, and the hosts of Heaven went forth glorifying God. Spiritual beings took their positions like pillars round about the upper chamber, and there came from above an ark of flame and fire which overshadowed the blessed Mother Mary.

213

The Angels began to sing, a light from above shone upon Mary's face as she lifted up her arms in a blessing. She heard a voice saying, "Thy holy soul shall rest in the kingdom of heaven where it shall find grace in joy and gladness. Welcome, blessed queen of women."

Her last words were the same as Jesus', "Father, into thy hands I commit my spirit."

Her soul left her body and in the silence that followed the fragrance of lily of the valley filled the chamber. (29.10)

Lord Jesus came to her on a cloud. The heavenly hosts accompanied the transfiguration with singing. All fell down and worshiped their Lord. Jesus blessed those present. Taking her soul, he held out his hand for Mary to join him, saying, "Come, my most precious pearl, enter into the way of eternal life. Come thou without fear for I am with thee. The heavenly host is waiting to bring thee into the joy of paradise.

Leaving her earthly body lying peacefully on her bed, Mary stepped into the chariot, and the heavenly voice welcomed her with, "This is my beloved daughter of whom I am well pleased." Accompanied by the Angels singing her praises, the cloud disappeared. And the Disciples saw her soul which was of great brightness and glistened.(29.11)

The laying down of the physical body by the power of Spirit involves the transmutation of its elements, hence it becomes invisible to mortal eyes. The blessed Virgin was the first and most advanced disciple of Christ. It was fitting therefore that she was the first to demonstrate this high attainment. The mystic Ceremonial of Death through which she passed was called the "Initiation of Earth." (29.12)

Jesus then instructed Peter to take Mary's body to the right-hand side of the city toward the east and place it in the new sepulcher.

The attending women prepared the body for burial and found that Mary's body had not aged. She looked like a young girl of sixteen, beautiful and as white as snow. It shone with such brightness they could hardly look upon it as they washed it. The sweet fragrance of the lily issued from it. They dressed it and placed it on the bier, The women accompanied the Disciples in the procession.

Placing her body on a bier covered with a canopy of light, the Disciples wrapped the body in a mantle of light, so the ancient legend relates, and they fastened the sides with that which resembled lightning. Above them all, thousands of Angels surrounded her, singing

215

praises to Mary the blessed one.

As they left the upper chamber John carried the glowing palm branch. (29.13)

The Shining Palm Leads the Way

It was then time for the Disciples to take the body to a safe place. With John leading the procession, holding aloft the sparkling palm branch, Peter lifted up his voice and began to sing:"Israel is Come out of Egypt, Allele." With sweet voices as the Angels in the clouds · overhead sang also.

The people of Bethlehem came out of their houses to see where the beautiful sound was coming from. They saw the bier and the procession walking along the road. Multitudes came to pay homage to the blessed Mary. (29.13)

Angry Pharisees Came

A group of angry (Pharisees) dissidents, one of them a prince of the priests of the Temple who had been searching for years to find the Mother Mary, descended upon the mourners, shouting loudly. The priest reached out with the intent to remove the body from the bier, but he was burned. As he reeled in agony, his arm stuck to the bier. He begged John to stop and release him. John challenged him to believe and be renewed in his spirit.

All those who were angry were instantly blinded by the Angels. Finally, Peter halted the procession and said to the suffering man, "If thou believest with thy whole heart in Jesus Christ, then your hands shall be loosed from the bier and healed." The priest, hardly able to speak said, "I believe, I believe all that thou sayest to me: only I beseech thee, have mercy on me let me loose lest I die."

John gave him the palm branch on the condition that for one week, he would go about the city of Jerusalem and heal all who needed healing. He promised to do so. He was instantly healed and released from the bier. He took up the shining palm branch and began healing all he passed. He went about the city healing the sick, a changed man. In a week he returned the shining palm branch to John.

Upon seeing this the crowd moved away and allowed the procession to proceed unhindered to Jerusalem.

It is said that the body of Mary remained in the tomb for three days. Her followers remained on watch. She still looked like she had as a young woman, though she was purported to be between fifty-two to sixty-five at her *passing.(29.14)*

There was a new cave near the Mount of Olives. In this cave they laid the body of Mary. Multitudes of people came to honor her. The sick or sorrowing came and were healed. (29.15)

Thomas' Story

(Assumption story: Joseph of Arimathaea) Thomas came late and related to them how he was saying mass in far away India, and he still had on his priestly vestments, when he was taken suddenly to the Mount of Olives to see the ascension of Mary. And he cried out to Mary. *"Make thy servant glad by thy mercy, for now thou goest away to heaven,"*

Mary loosened the girdle (belt) which the Apostles had put around her waist and she threw it down to him. He took it and went to the valley of Josaphat near Mary's tomb, where he greeted the Apostles.

Peter critically announced, *"Thou wast always unbelieving, and so the Lord hath not suffered thee to be at his mother's burial."*

To which he replied, *"I know I have been unbelieving. I ask pardon of you all,"* and they prayed for him.

218

Finally, he asked," *Where have you laid her body?"* They pointed to the sepulcher. *"Her holy body is not there."* he replied.

Peter said, *"Thou wast always unbelieving, so the Lord hath not allowed thee to be at his mothers' burial."*

Thomas was adamant saying: *"She is not there."* They took away the stone from the tomb, and the body was not there; and they were speechless. .

Thomas told them that he had witnessed Mary's ascension with Jesus at her side, and she had given him her girdle (belt); he held up her belt for them to see.

They all rejoiced and begged his pardon. He blessed them and said: *"Behold how good and pleasant a thing it is, brethren, to dwell together in unity."* On further examination of the sepulcher they found beautifully blooming roses growing inside the tomb and the scent of Lily of the Valley permeated the area.

The disciples had experienced the great joy and up lifting of Mary's transfiguration and each one returned to his mission with greater wisdom and unity than ever before. Each of the disciples was returned in a cloud the

same way they were brought to the Assumption of the Mother Mary.
(Pseudo Molenta)

Chapter 30

The Mysteries

The secret keys to the mysteries are placed within the biblical records of the lives of the followers of the Christ which to the initiated reader indicate the specific Degree to which they have progressed and which, moreover, serve to outline the process of development for the esoteric aspirant who seeks to take the Way of the Cross and to follow the Path of Christian Discipleship.

In common with the Ancient Mysteries, the Greater Mysteries inaugurated by the Christ are divided into three principal steps or Degrees. The first is the Rite of Purification, which is concerned with the cleansing of the lower nature of the sense life. In the Rite of Purification, the neophyte is taught how to live a chaste and harmless life. As the aspirant remains true to the principles in this Degree it leads to the beginning of what is called 'living the Christ life.'

Every step on the Path carries with it a spiritual compenstation. The First Degree allows the Initiate to serve as a conscious Invisible Helper. (Light Bearer).

The Second Degree is the Rite of Illumination or enlightenment and pertains to the etheric body, that awakens the power of positive clairvoyance and clairaudience. With the coming of the Christ this was introduced by means of concentration or will be taken from the masculine pole of Spirit as active prayer. Plus the practice of meditation from the feminine pole, or imagination used as the listening process. By means of these activities the centers of the desire body overcome the barrier to higher spiritual attainment.

The Third Degree is that of Mastership which unites the etheric and the desire bodies to create a medium by which the illumined Spirit attains the Mystic Marriage of personality. The forces of the personal self have been sublimated to enter the perfect union with Spirit. Heaven and earth unite to honor this Master.

This Degree is concealed in the story of the marriage at Cana in Galilee with which John opens his Gospel. This marriage is recorded as occurring on the "third day." The word Cana means "to heal"

Elevated Masters experience no separation between inner and outer planes, nor limitations between life and death, thus they are able to enjoy the sublime state of eternal consciousness.

Light Bodies

The higher life essences or Light Bodies, accumulated in past lives are drawn about the head of a child at birth; these form the halo usually represented about the heads of Jesus, Mary, Joseph, John the Baptist, Samuel, and the saints. Through love and service these ethers gradually form into the "wedding garment" which encircles the entire body. The greater the accumulated soul powers from the past, the sooner this garment of the soul is fashioned in the present life. The teachings in the Temple marked the mature development of the soul body of Jesus. He realized then that the serious work of his ministry had begun: *"Wist ye not that I must be about my Father's business?"* Special work had to be done to refine and accelerate the vibratory power of the blood, even in a body as pure as that of Jesus, in order that it might become a fitting vehicle for the great Christ Spirit.

Mary kept all these things in her heart, and in the full flood-tide of realization which was hers after the illumination of Pentecost, she gave them to Luke, who has recorded all with rare and tender delicacy in his Gospel.(30.1)

The Mysteries of Mary and Joseph

Mary represents the Love Power of the soul raised from bondage to liberation in Spirit. She symbolizes the perfect completion of the inner work which we all must attain through the pathways of Sorrow and Joy which is considered the most difficult way, but the fastest.

Each individualization incarnates alternately in male and female bodies, and experiences are blended to constitute *"The major and minor chords of the symphony of life."* All life experiences are a preparation for Initiation.

Life is the great Teacher. No two persons have the same experiences. The fourteen steps outlined are fundamental to the total of the seven primary Initiatory Degrees mastered by this Holy couple in the bringing forth of the great Light, the Christ of God.

Mary and Joseph, because of their high attainment, passed through certain experiences as referred to by early Christians *"The path of the Seven Sorrows and the Seven Joys."* The Sorrows represent the learning experiences of daily life in the world often disciplinary in nature to develop self-discipline. The Joys nourish the soul and increase faith while living the worldly life.

Both Sorrows and Joys are needed for development of the soul. The Joys and Sorrows of life are kept at a perfect balance.

These Sorrows and Joys are a part of the life experience (education) of every person who follows this path which culminate in high levels of consciousness according to the Laws of Karma and the Laws of Love.(30.2)

The Seven Sorrows of Joseph were:
1. *Leaving Mary*
2. *No place for the Nativity but in a manger.*
3. *The suffering of the Holy Child in circumcision.*
4. *Simeon's prophecy of sorrow for Mary.*
5. *The flight into Egypt.*
6. *Fear of Herod's son on the return to Nazareth.*
7. *Loss of the young Jesus in Jerusalem.*

The Seven Joys of Joseph:
1. *Angelic communication of the Incarnation*
2. *Adoration of the Shepherds.*
3. *The naming of Jesus*
4. *Adoration of the Wise Men*
5. *Simeon's pronouncement of the coming salvation through Jesus, the Christ.*
6. *The angelic summons to return from Egypt.*
7. *Finding Jesus in the Temple in Jerusalem.*

The Seven Sorrows of Mary:
1. The prophecy of Simeon.
2. The flight into Egypt.
3. The three days' loss of the boy Jesus in Jerusalem.
4. Meeting Jesus with the cross.
5. The Crucifixion
6. The removal of Jesus from the cross.
7. The Holy burial.

The Seven Joys of Mary:
1. The Annunciation
2. The Nativity
3. The Purification
4. Finding Jesus in the Temple after three days.
5. The Resurrection.
6. The Descent of the Holy Ghost at Pentecost.
7. The Assumption   (30-3)

Esoteric Meaning of the Path to Illumination

Feminine Initiates have been closely linked with the divine mysteries of Virgo, the constellation in the heavens which is represented by the Virgin bearing a sheaf of wheat. The key words of this subtle work are *Immaculate Conception....*

There are three levels leading to Infinite Wisdom. The first is Mary, the second Jesus and the third God. Without Mary, the Christ

within cannot be born. The importance of Mary in the spiritual life of the world will become increasingly paramount in the present Aquarian Age as the province of woman, with the prerogatives of the heart, receive greater emphasis." (30.4)
Mary of Bethlehem was chosen by the Masters who guide human evolution for the task of bringing to earth the holy Mysteries of the Immaculate Conception. From her home in the angelic realms she labors unceasingly for the spiritual illumination of all women. (30.5)

The Path of the Heart has been crowned by the wondrous light of Mary; called the Queen of Hearts. St. Francis of Assisi, in his ecstatic Initiatory vision saw the Path, symbolized by a great ladder extending into heaven; at the very top the Blessed Virgin was standing.(30.6)

Walt Whitman, seer-poet, paid fitting tribute to the spirit of womanhood when he said:
"Woman, be not dismayed.
Thy task encompasseth all.
Thou art the gateway of the body.
Thou art the gateway of the soul." (30.7)

It is recorded that God made an assemblage of all the waters and called it the sea (Mare). He made an assemblage of all the graces and called it Mary (Maria). The sea is the universal symbol of the psychic or emotional nature. To calm, lift and transmute is the purpose of the Water, or Heart Initiation. Mary was also called the Star of the Sea.

Woman was first to receive and understand the glorious truth of Resurrection; she, too, will be first to receive and interpret the Mysteries and Truths belonging to the New Age and to the pioneers of this New Day.

Mary, Mother of Light travels the bridge of unification between East and West. From this unification will come the rarest spiritual treasure the world has known: the emancipation of woman. (30.8)

Initiates
Who Advanced as a Result of the Holy Birth

<u>Cousin Elizabeth</u> who sheltered Mary in her home in Hebron during her pregnancy

<u>The two midwives Zalome and Salome</u> became Initiates as a result of their participation in the birth.

<u>The shepherds</u> present at the birth of the Holy Babe were said to be neophytes who had achieved the Degree of Purification and were in communion with Beings of celestial realms

who told them to come unto the Star, to adore the Holy Child. (30.9)

The shepherdess advanced as a result of her kindness to the Holy family.

The Wise Men had passed the First and Second Degrees of the Christ Mysteries. They came with their gifts, symbolizing the overcoming of their physical levels, and were spiritualized in Body and Mind, creating their radiant bodies of light. It was said that three persons in glowing white robes attended the birth. This is the "golden wedding garment" that each disciple must wear in the presence of the Christ.(30.10)

Mary of Bethlehem, Virgin Mother of the Christos, leader in the early church A strong supporter of women and children, holds forth the Eternal Light of Love and Truth. She attained the Archangel status and became Queen of the Angels.

Those Who Assisted Mary In Her Life

Salome: first midwife called who recognized the Christ and announced Mary's virginity.
Zalome: second midwife who challenged Mary's virginity.
The Shepardess advanced as a result of her

Mary of Cleothis Mary, sister of the Virgin, Mother of James and Jude. Came to the tomb. Was present at the crucifixion and may have become a missionary to whom Jesus appeared as she and her husband were walking along a road, She was also a strong supporter of the early church. Mary's family were a closely-knit,highly spiritual family, probably Essene. Many became followers of Jesus and are mentioned in various places.
Calietha, daughter of Nicodemus.
Neshra, daughter of Gamaliel.
Veronica, who wiped the Master's brow on the way to Golgotha.
Mary Magdala, Most advanced of the apostles. Present at the foot of the Cross, she came to the empty tomb in preparation for entering the Mystic Death and experiencing the illumination that follows the Rite of the Resurrection.
Salome, came to the tomb also, where they were met by two Angels representing the purified body
Joanna, wife of Herod's steward, Chuza. Came to the tomb.
Received Complete Resurrection Bodies:These four women reached greater attainment as they went on to Galilee according to the Zohar where they received complete resurrection bodies: Mary of Cleothis, the Virgins sister, Mary of Magdela, Salome, and Joanna. (30.11)

Tabitha, daughter of Archelaus present at Mary's death and may have prepared her body for burial.

Other women present at her Assumption:
Sepphora, Abigea and Zael
Mary's Family :
Disciples John, James his brother, Peter, Paul, Andrew, Philip, Luke, Barnabas, Bartholomew, Matthew, Matthias surnamed Justus, Simon the Canaanite, Jude and his brother, Nicodemus, Maximianus
Anna-Hanna was Mary's mother who bore her as a result of an immaculate conception-without an earthly father.
Virgin Mary's Father: Joachim-Highly evolved-golden Wedding Garment.
Elizabeth:Mary's cousin who gave birth at an advanced age to John the Baptist. She was the wife of Zachariah.
Grandmother: Faustina.

It is fitting that the idea of equality of all people be presented by Mary. Her example of love,caring of all reminds us that it's eternally possible.

Chapter 31

Mary Begins Her Heavenly Mission

After the Assumption, the Virgin Mary lived in the realm of the Angels. Upon viewing what the future held for the earth and its inhabitants, she chose to remain nearby the earth in order to prepare the human race for its next steps, called "the coming age of Mary" or the Venus period."

The Venus Period is described in esoteric language as an advanced stage of development of the physical body into a finer vehicle; and, desire itself will become Light. In describing a beautiful scene, the human mind through pictures will be able to communicate it to others, and the person talked to will be able to see the scene through his mind as if he is present looking at it.

The Aquarian Age is described as the time when Heaven and Earth come closer together than ever before. Many wonderful miracles and much change is the result. The Mother Mary is preparing humanity to take the greatest advantage of these healing events.

Mother Mary works on behalf of the feminine principle. The idea that all human beings hold the two aspects of masculine and feminine within themselves is the beginning.

Throughout this work in presenting the esoteric values of the sacred Scripture of Christendom we have emphasized the importance of the feminine attributes of selflessness, love, constancey intuition and imagination: a deep regard for the advancement of soul individually and collectively. Let it be clear that our regard for Mary is of an impersonal nature, that we are primarily concerned with the Divine Feminine in all humanity. Mary certainly is the fine example of this so far in this world. (31.1)

Mary, the Cosmic Madonna, belongs to no church, or creed. Her work encompasses all races, all humanity.

The Mother Mary renounced what could have been her high estate in order to remain close to the earth plane to assist in the evolution of humankind to the next initiatory state.
Each conflict one sees in the world should be looked upon as a step in evolution, the fine tuning of all humanity bringing into view the Venus period.

The Mother Mary is preparing the world to be freed from the old way of prejudice, judgement and non-forgiveness. Hate, fear, guilt and the belief that there is only way will be discarded.

All people of the earth will live together in harmony, caring for one another in love, peace and respect.

The Virgin Mary has shown herself hundreds of times in the past, and because this earth is so dear to her heart, she will no doubt be seen many more times in the future. Her work becomes more visible as more people question the old way and seek to find answers for the future.

Because many seekers are preparing themselves for Initiation into the Mysteries, Mary was chosen to provide the high lessons of the Degree of Adeptship--the Descent of the Holy Ghost--the blending of the two paths of Fire and Water, head and heart.

"To place and keep oneself in alignment with Spiritual Law is the only method wherby life pays just dividends on either the physical or higher planes." (31.2)

It is fitting that the idea of equality of all people be presented by Mary. Her example of love and caring of all reminds us that it is eternally possible.

The Mother Mary and her Angels are always

available for consultation and wisdom. One need only ask.

End thought: The Ways

To every man there openth
The Way, and Ways, and a Way,
And the High Soul Climbs the High Way
And the Low Soul gropes the Low,
And in between, on the misty flats,
The rest drift to and fro.
But to every man there openeth
A High way and a Low.
And every man decideth
The Way his soul shall go.

by John Oxenham

GLOSSARY

Abaddon: Angel of Destruction. Mentioned at Joseph's death.

Angel: Angels are our spiritual perceptual faculties, which dwell in the presence of the Father. (Matt.13:49) "There Angels do always behold the face of my Father who is in heaven." Their responsibilities are to guard, guide and direct the natural forces of mind and body which have in them the future of all beings, individually and collectively. (G.1)

Akashic Records: aka. God's Book of Remembrance, The place where the history and wisdom of all the generations of humankind is recorded. Anna and Simeon, both Temple Initiates possessed the ability to read the Akashic Records. Cosmic Scrolls contain an outline of the past, present and future of the human race. This Cosmic Scroll Mary described as a *"lofty pillar of gold covered all over with inscriptions."*

St. John saw the sublime vision of the woman clothed with the sun, her feet upon the moon and crowned with the glory of the twelve stars. The disciples and their students were also privileged to read the Akashic Records.

Raphael was privileged to view the Akashic

Records when he was painting the Sistine Madonna.

Anna-Hanna: Mary's mother. Daughter of Faustina. Her birth and Mary's were considered Immaculate Conceptions.

Annunciation: In Biblical terms, *annunciation* is an announcement given to the conscious mind regarding the answer to prayer, often by an angelic revelation.

Annunciation is also a process enacted within the body of every neophyte male or female. He/she becomes conscious, after a certain period of preparation, that particular changes are taking place within himself, due to an accumulation of the essences (ethers) and the acceleration of the vibratory rate of his/her entire being.

Assumption: Mary's death as a legend of transportation of the soul of the Virgin to Heaven by Jesus, the Christ and his Angels followed by the disappearance of her body into a dense cloud. Some had thought she suffered martyrdom. Epiphanies was uncertain as to whether she died and was buried.(G.2)

Books: of James and Thomas were attributed

to second century writers. Origen mentioned this might mean that Mary was present in Joseph's family and partially raised James a son from Joseph's former marriage In this case she could have had some tie to him when she desired to see Jesus later in his ministry. James claimed to have been present at Jesus' birth in a cave These stories were included in Origen's writings. He died in 254 CE.

On the cross Jesus realized that none of the men of his household were present so he gave custody of the Virgin Mary to his closest friend, John.

Brethren of the Lord: Jesus' Family: Epiphanian,
The brethren of Jesus were the children of
Joseph by a former wife and were older than
Jesus.

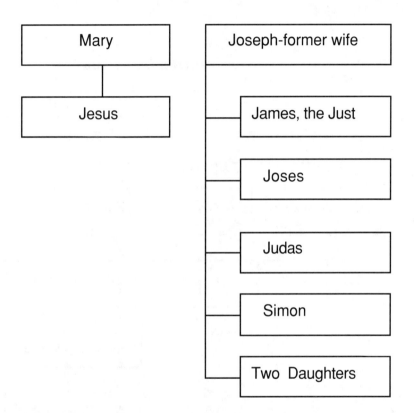

Mary's Familly
The Proevangelion Chapter XIII: *1 And leaving
her {Mary} and his sons in the cave, Joseph
went forth to seek a Hebrew midwife in the
village of Bethlehem.* This would imply that
more than one son accompanied Joseph and

Mary to Bethlehem and that they were older than Jesus. Could the youngest have been James the Just? In this case he would have been older than Jesus and possibly younger than Mary. He would have been Joseph's youngest son.

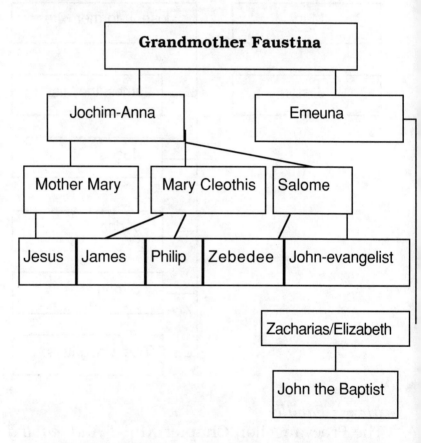

Helvidian View: That the brothers and sisters of Jesus were the children of Joseph and Mary, younger than Jesus. Thus Mary did not remain a virgin.

Jesus' Family: Jerome: that the brethren of Jesus were not brothers but cousins. The two daughters names were Assia and Lydia "The assumption necessary for this theory was that "brethren" meant cousins. Still held by some Roman Catholics." (G.3)2.

Essenes: A highly esoteric group related to the Great White Brotherhood of Egypt. Women were highly respected. When they were pregnant they had no duties other than providing the incoming spirit with a suitable body through which to function. During this time they ate nothing unclean nor engaged in any worldly activity. The importance of the divine feminine, was stressed in many of the pre-Christian religions.

Feast of the Assumption: August 15, (Catholic, Eastern Orthodox) Commemorates the departure of the Virgin Mary from this life and her assumption into Heaven. A Catholic Holy Day of Obligation in the Catholic Church

Female role: Women in the middle east at that time were considered unclean and unable to attain a place in Heaven. She was restrained from speaking in the presence of a man other than her husband. For example:
(*Gospel of Thomas, the Complete Gospel, Miller p.322)* This took place when the Master was defending Mary Magdalene at a meeting

with the disciples. Evidently, Mary Magdalene and the Mother Mary were present.vs.114

Simon Peter said to them, "Make Mary leave us, for females don't deserve life." Jesus said,"Look, I will guide her to make her like us, so that she too may become a living spirit resembling you. For every female who lifts herself up will enter the domain of Heaven."

Referred in both Thomas 114 and Gospel of Mary Magdalene vs.109) This implies that the Master considered her to be worthy based on her having achieved a supreme spiritual state, or "truly human." (Gospel of Philip 63;34--) *"Why do you love her more than us? Jesus answered, "Why do I not love you like her?" (G.4)*

After the resurrection,the Mother Mary, the disciples and Mary of Magdalene met together in a locked room as they were afraid of their adversaries. The Master visited them and charged them to go out into the world and preach the gospel.

After he left them they began weeping and wailing about how they might do this when Mary of Magdalene stood and addressed them saying that *some of what she had learned might not be known to them.* (What she said is missing from the script.) *When she had*

finished she sat in silence, symbolizing the
perfect rest of the soul set free. (Coptic 10:1-
10)

"Then Andrew answered, addressing the
brothers, "Say what you will about the truth of
the things she has said, but I do not believe
that the Savior said these things. For indeed
these teachings are strange ideas!"

Peter's questions were: *"Did Jesus speak with*
a woman in private without our knowing about
it? Are we to turn around and listen to her? Did
he choose her over us?"

Mary Magdelene wept. Then she said to Peter,
"My brother, what are you imagining about
this?"Do you think that I've made all this up by
myself or that I am telling lies about the
Savior?"

Levi said to Peter, "Peter, you have a constant
inclination to anger and you are always ready
to give way to it. And even now you are doing
exactly that by questioning the woman as if
you're her enemy. If the Savior considered her
to be worthy, who are you to disregard her? For
he knew her completely and loved her
devotedly."(8)

This common belief concerning the
spirituality of women has changed very little

in the Middle East in two thousand years. She would not be eligible to attain the same spiritual level of under- standing that a male could. It was believed that the female had no soul and therefore could not enter Heaven.

Mary of Magdalene proved that she was more spiritually advanced than most of the Disciples; this was acknowledged by the Master Jesus. According to the Hebrew teaching, Heaven was not available to a woman. Mary of Magdalene was his most accomplished student.(G.4)

First born: does not imply that Mary ever bore another child. This title among the Jews belonged to an only child (if a son) to mark his rights and duties under the Law. This word does not deny Mary's life time virginity. (G.5)

Girdle/belt. Thomas was late to the Annunciation of Mary, it is said that as she was being lifted up, she saw him and dropped her girdle to him.(G.6)

Golden Gate : This is a mystical reference to the states of soul exaltation in which Anna and Joachim experienced during the sacred time of imaculate conception. Filled with holy ecstasy, a cloud of light enfolded them and they were luminous with a great shining.

Angels encircled them with songs of great joy. It is a gate in the walls of Jerusalem. (G.6)

Grotto or Cave: Jesus who was called Joseph until he reached the time of his ministry, was born in a cave or grotto that had been prepared for them by the Essenes who maintained a hospital or hospice house on the outskirts of Bethlehem. Built into hollowed out caves were many rooms that were free from moisture, dampness, heat or cold. Some were covered with mud cement and decorated artistically. It was quite common for women to have their babies there. Finding a midwife in attendance was not unexpected.(G.7)

Holy Spirit: The Archangel Michael was called to be the Mother of Jesus and was referred to as the Holy Spirit. first by Cyril of Jerusalem (4th century) and later by Jerome(4-5th century)

Jesus said, "Just now my mother, the Holy Spirit, took me by one of my hairs and brought me to Mt. Tabor, the great mountain." Comment: The Holy Spirit talks more like divine wisdom instead of the devil who tempted him on Mt. Tabor.(G.9) Origen,3rd Century)

Immaculate Conception: Refers to the pure and Immaculate conception of Anna, the mother of Mary and to Mary herself, by her Holy parents Joachim and Anna as Angels procreate by mutual meeting of soul to soul. The babe was presented to her arms, leaving the mother a virgin.(G.9)

Initiation : Conscious immortality is the supreme gift of Initiation. Each level of initiation attained is acknowledged in some way. The Master Jesus was acknowledged at the River Jordan, through Baptism, and transfiguration on the Mount when his disciples were present and at his Resurrection. This ceremony is performed so that the Initiate knows that he knows. This is conscious immortality.

Feast of Transfiguration: Aug 6 (Protestant, Catholic, Eastern Orthodox) Celebrates the occasion when Jesus led Peter, James and John up a mountain, where his physical appearance changed and he was bathed in light. A voice spoke saying, *"This is my beloved Son, in whom I am well pleased."*(G.10)

Jerome: a.d. 4-5 lived and studied for thirty years in Bethlehem in preparation for his version of the Bible (Latin Vulgate), and had access to many ancient manuscripts that described the Holy Family. i.e.The physical description of Mother Mary as a girl.

(Anonymous.*The Lost Books of the Bible*.(Ameridian Book.New American Library.1926 (G.11) *Gospel of the Birth of Mary* by Jerome).

Jesus or Joseph: He may have been given the name Joseph at his circumcision, and he may have used it later during his Mt. Carmel College years and/or later as he traveled about as a tutor /translator for the Egyptian trader.

The original Hebrew name Jesus meant, helped of Yahweh, or, later, to deliver or to save. "Savior" was a natural useage.(G.12)

Jesus- the name: Our pronunciation of the name "Jesus" comes directly from the Greek. But the true name is Aramaic and not Greek. It is pronounced Eshoa originating from Hebrew Yehoshua meaning "Yahweh saves, helps or aids." Most New Testament scholars believe it more precisely means "Yahweh, help !" rather than "Yahweh helps or saves." Aramaic and Hebrew are sister languages.

Much of Hebrew comes directly from Aramaic. Our English word Christ comes from Greek Christos, which is a translation from Aramaic m'sheeha meaning "the anointed, appointed, or ordained one." The root of the word means "to anoint, with oil and to enlighten." The Messiah was to carry the "light" of God, that is, anointed to do God's work. (G.13)

Kundalini: (Spirit-Fire.) Mysteries of the Fire-Mist. When the divine creative essence, light force passes up the spinal cord, the true path of discipleship, and reaches the head, it illuminates two spiritual organs located therein, the pineal body and the pituitary gland, and they shine with rare radiance. With this accomplished, the disciple then bears within himself his own lighted lamp and is ever ready to welcome the Bride groom. (G.14)

Letter to Mother Mary
from Jesus on the Death of Joseph

Messengers from Galilee brought the news that Joseph had died and that Mary was unconsoled. "Beloved Mother: Be not grieved, for all is well for Father as with you. He has completed his present work here on earth, and has done so nobly. None in any walk of life can charge him with deceit, dishonesty, nor wrong intention. In his period of life here he has completed many great tasks and is gone from our midst truly prepared to solve the problems that await him in the future. Our God, the

248

Father of all of us, is with him now as He was with him heretofore; but even now the Heavenly Hosts guard his footsteps and protect him on his way. Therefore, why should you weep and suffer? Tears will not conquer your grief, and your sorrow cannot be vanquished by any emotion of your heart or mind. Let your soul be busy in meditation and contact with him who is gone, and if thou art not idle, there will be no time for grief. When grief throbs through the heart, and anguish causes you pain, permit yourself to rise to higher planes and indulge in the ministry of love.

Your ministry has always been that of love, and in the Brotherhood thou canst find many opportunities to answer the call of the world for more love. Therefore, let the past remain the past. Rise above the cares of earthly things and give your life to those who still live with us here on earth. When your life is done, you will find it again in the morning sun, or even in the evening dew, as in the song of birds, the perfume of the flowers, and the mystic lights of the stars at night.

For it will not be long before your problems and toils here on earth will be solved also, and when all is counted and arranged, you will be ready for greater fields of effort and prepared to solve the greater problems of the soul. Try, then, to be content until I come to you soon and bring to you richer gifts than those made of gold or precious stones. I am sure that my brothers will care for you and supply your needs, and I am always with you in mind and spirit. Your son, Joseph (Joseph was the name that Jesus used in school.(G.15)

Madonna: My lady. Often refers to the paintings of the Mother Mary. Raphael painted many madonnas. Raphael was a great master of the Mystical Brotherhood and used his vision of the Akashic records to pattern his painting of the Madonna. He painted the Sistine Madonna, considered the greatest masterpiece of its kind, which has been purported to have great healing powers. Books have been written chronicling the history of the Sistine Madonna, of the many miracles and the strong impression it has upon its viewers.

Magi: The Magi referred to in the Bible were not simply astrologers, or Kings, but were the learned instructors and high representatives of the great academies and the Mystery Schools of the Orient. The title of "Magus" was granted only to one who had attained the very high degree of initiation in the Mystery Schools, and who were masters of the arts and sciences, as well as highly evolved mystics.

The Magi were consulted by kings, potentates, and learned people of all lands, not only in regard to matters of astrology or astronomy, but in regard to matters of state, history, medicine, natural law, spiritual law: subjects that required profound thinking.

The Magi knew well the story of Mary as the chosen mother of the Holy Child, the location of Joseph's home in Nazareth and the arrangement of going to the Essene grotto hospice of the Brotherhood near Bethlehem. The Magi were close at hand in Jerusalem when the Star reached its zenith and began to suddenly descend. They knew that the time had come for the Holy Birth.

Besides the items mentioned in the Bible, they brought greetings from the Great White Brotherhood, jewels of a symbolic nature for the mother and father, and a rosary containing a rare emblem identifying Jesus as the anticipated Son of God.(G.16)

Other accounts record that the ancient books of Seth, the son of Adam, were also given. (G.17)

The Magi, after having made their official visit, journeyed on to Mt. Carmel, the Mystery School, and made their report. They gave instructions for the education and care of the child throughout his infancy and childhood. Then they traveled on to Egypt and made their report to the High Priests and the Supreme officers of the Great White Brotherhood (White Light). (G.18)

The Manger of Light: The pineal gland crowns the masculine or fire column,(Joseph) the pituitary gland crowns the feminine, water-column, (Mary). The combination of the two becomes the manger of Light. It cannot be given to anyone. It must be woven by the initiates themselves. This is the method of building the etheric bodies through the dedication of the self to service to others. This is available to all people. (G.19)

Mary's Parents: Two different accounts were given: 1. Both parents died while she was serving in the Temple.(G.20)

Mary's Mother, Anna: 2. After the death of Joachim, Anna, a most beautiful and wealthy woman, and still must have been of child bearing age, may have married a man named Clethis, and had yet another daughter.(G.21) The traditional marriage age for men was thirty and for women after the age of twelve. So, Anna was still of child bearing age.

It was important in that day for a woman to be married as women had few rights to property, and it was dangerous for her to live alone. Some financial provision was required to care for each of Joachim's children. Mary, being the elder probably inherited the greatest amount to become a very wealthy woman. She was definitely one to be sought after for many reasons.

Miraculous Conception: The conception of the child Jesus without the assistance of a mortal father, by the direct power of God. Described as: the "Holy Spirit came upon me." The babe was carried in Mary's womb for seven months and both she and Jesus contributed to making the body strong and healthy. Mary was still a virgin after the birth as verified by the midwife. (G.22)

Mount Carmel College: The Essenes maintained a college, school, and Monastery at Mount Carmel which Jesus entered. Joseph ben Joseph a young mystic from Galilee regarded by some as being Jesus also studied and taught there. Jesus was recognized by these Great White Brotherhood teachers as already an advanced student from the beginning of his time there. He studied and taught for a number of years under the directions of the Master Teachers.

Later he was sent to visit the centers of learning throughout the world to study. Many records of a Joseph ben Joseph, have been found in the Rosicrucian Library.The Magi stopped at Mt. Carmel after visiting the Holy Family in Bethlehem to prepare the way for Jesus' education. Former students were such notables as Elijah and his son, Elisha.

Accounts of Jesus' journey are also found in Urantia transmitted records. He accompanied as a tutor, a wealthy Egyptian youth whose father was a traveling tradesman welcome in the courts of nobles in the known world. He may have been using the name Joseph ben Joseph instead of Jesus.This translator was of Hebrew lineage and fluent in five languages.Through these connections he met learned persons of the world (G.23)

Nazarene: According to Rosicrucian records which predate Jesus, the Christ, he was a Galilean of Gentile parentage and an Aryan, by blood. Gentiles by natural religious classification, mystics by philosophical thought, and Jews by forced adoption. As the Gentiles of Galilee after 103 B.C. were forced to adopt circumcision and respect the Mosaic law, and in accordance with this law all children at a certain age had to accept the Jewish faith by appearing at the Temple in Jerusalem for admission to the church.

Nazareth: According to Rosicrution writings there never was nor is there now as one travels through the Holy Land a place marked where Jesus grew up. There was a Nazarene sect considered heretic by the Pharisees who had settlements on the banks of Lake Galilee. According to more ancient records they were Aryans from Egypt who spoke yet another language. Though effort was made to prove by family lineage that Joseph was descended from King David, other sources claim that was not the case. He was Aryan, fair skinned and blue eyed. Only one source listed him as a Nazarene or Jesus of Nazareth.(G.24)

Origen: 185-253 a.d. Early Greek philosopher from Alexandria who held that Neoplatonism and Christianity were compatable. *"The Holy Spirit talks like divine wisdom in stead of the devil who tempted him on Mt. Tabor.*(Origen (3rd Century)

Prophetess of the Temple: Various names used from different sources were: Hannah, Anna and Anne, who blessed the babe Jesus and prophesied about his life. She may have also been Mary's teacher during her service in the Temple.

Public Settlements in the Temple: Mary may have been a ward of the Temple. This meaning that they managed her inheritance from her father's estate. The High Priest ordered that all virgins of the Temple who held public settlements must leave. This was one cause of the young Mary's leaving the Temple service.The other was she was growing up and would defile the Temple.(G.25)

Rite of Purification After Child Birth: *And the Lord spoke unto Moses and said to him.*
2. Speak to the children of Israel saying. If a woman has conceived and born a male child, then she shall be unclean seven days; according to the days of her menstruation she shall be unclean.
3. And on the eighth day the flesh of his foreskin shall be circumcised.
4. And she shall continue for thirty-three days in the blood of her purifying; she shall touch no hallowed thing, nor come into the sanctuary, until the days of her purifying be fulfilled.
5. But if she bears a female child, then she shall be unclean two weeks, as in her menstruation; and she shall continue in the blood of her purifying for sixty-six days.
6. And when the days of her purifying are fulfilled for a son or a daughter, she shall bring a lamb of the first year for a burnt offering and a young pigeon or a turtle dove for a sin offering to the door of the tabernacle, of the congregation, to the priest.
7. And he shall offer it before the Lord and

make an atonement for her; and she shall be cleansed from the issue of her blood. This is the law for her who has born a male child or a female.
8. And if she cannot afford a lamb, then she shall bring two pigeons or two young turtle doves; the one for the sin offering and the other for the burnt offering; and the priest shall make an atonement for her and she shall be clean..(G.26)

The scripture tells that Mary gave two turtle doves as her offering for her cleansing signifying to some translators that they were a poor family.

Robes of Aaron-Fountlet: The fountlet is purported to be a golden plate that reflected and revealed the image of the persons consciousness to him. It may be tied with purple ribbons attached to a head band or miter. *Exodus 28:36. And you put it on blue lace, that it may be upon the mitre (fountlet); ...And it shall be upon Aaron's forehead and Aaron shall bear the sins of the children of Israel when they shall offer holy sacrifices and all their holy gifts; and the mitre shall be always upon his forehead, that they may be accepted before the Lord. (G,27)*

An instrument , a plate which God had appointed the high-Priest to wear for the followers to look into and discover if they had sinned. (1) i.e. Joachim looked into the shiny fountlet worn by the priest and saw that he was without sin.

Salome: Second midwife to arrive. Remembered from an early painting. (See insert plates) When she held the babe she swore to follow him through out his life. She became a disciple of Mary and did great deeds of benefit to many people. (G.28)

Surviving Children's Death Benefits:
According to Hebrew Law,(Five daughters of Zelopohehad case) remaining daughters, when there were no sons, could inherit the father's fortune if they married within the tribe.

Job made arrangements that all his children, seven boys and two girls share in his fortune when he died at the age of 140 years. "And he gave them (his daughters) an inheritance among their brothers. (Job 42:13-16) i.e. When Joachim died Mary was still serving in the Temple. He was a wealthy man.

According to the Law his daughters could inherit his property. He had two daughters, Mary who was serving in the Temple and Mary who was very young. His property would have been divided between the two leaving nothing for his wife, Anna. The Temple priests became the administrators of Mary's estate.(G.29)

The Star: We must not presume that the Magi observed the Star only a few hours before the birth of the Holy Child and hurriedly set out to follow it. It was sighted, according to many accounts, weeks before the birth by Magi from far different lands who journeyed to be present at the birth.(G.30)

The Urantian explanation was that Jesus was born at noon on August 21, 7 B.C. and an extraordinary conjunction of Jupiter and Saturn occurred on May 29, September 29 and December 5 of that year. The babe was three weeks old by the time the wise men came to him. (13)

Johannes Kepler (1571-1630) observed the conjunction of Jupiter and Saturn in 1603 and determined that it was possible that Jupiter and Saturn may have been in conjunction in 7 BCE.

Four duplicate cuneiform scripts impressed into clay that may have been Balthassar's Almanac, an amazingly rare find from ancient Babylonia and inscribed dating to 8 B.C.E.predicted three conjunctions of Saturn and Jupiter during the year 7/6 B.C.E. in the constellation of Pisces.

The new year began at the vernal equinox March/April. The Three conjunctions were in May, October and December. The scripts indicates that at the December conjunction Mars had also moved into Pisces. If the Magi came from Babylon it would have been at least a two-month journey. If they left at the second sighting, they would have arrived just as or about the time of a December first birth date. (G,31) (Ideas taken from Bible Review Magazine 12/02)

Many other notables have had a star announce their impending birth. Buddha, Confucius 551 B.C. Mithras, (the Persian Savior) Socrates, Aesculapius, Bacchus, Romulus, and many others.

The esoteric teachings say that the light was not a star at all, but an Angel perhaps Gabriel glowing day and night to lead the Magi to the holy birth place.(G.32)

Systematic Stages for rearing Hebrew children:
They divided the child's life into seven stages.
1. The newborn child, the first to eighth day. Boys circumcised
2. The suckling child.
3. The weaned child.
4. The period of dependence on the mother,

lasting through the fifth year.

5. The beginning independence of the child and, with sons, the father assuming responsibility for their education. Girls training for marriage.

6. Boys at age seven were entered into the local Synagogue schools already a fluent reader, writer and speaking Aramaic and Greek. From age ten years until age thirteen they studied the rudiments of the Book of Law in Hebrew. Graduating then, they were considered a "son of the commandment" and responsible citizens of Israel which required their attendance at Passover the following year.

7.Adolescent boys: Temple examination-Bar Mitzva. Girls - marriage. Generally not educated.

8. Young men: Learned a trade.Young women became mothers.

It was common for Hebrew boys to be able to read, write and speak in three languages: Aramaic, Greek, and Hebrew.

Joseph spoke Greek and taught his sons from the Scriptures in Greek presented to them in Alexandria before they left Egypt.(G.33)

Several school texts have survived written on papyri, ostraca, and wooden tablets.(G.34)

The Title of the Christ: Jesus is the historical name. Christ, the equivalent of Messiah, anointed one is the title of his office. The two names were not generally used together as a proper name until after the Ascension. (G.35)

The Temple: : May not have always meant the Hebrew Temple at Jerusalem. It may have been referring to the Essene Temple in Jerusalem which was mentioned in the Rosicrucian documents. Some of the references in the Bible may have been to the local meeting place in Nazareth. If Mary and Joseph made as many trips to Jerusalem as stated in these documents they would have been traveling most of the time.

Temple Veil: The Temple Veil was to be made and the virgins were called. The division of work was chosen by lot. Mary's lot was to spin and weave the scarlet and the purple not the veil. When Jesus was crucified it is said that the veil of the Temple was torn asunder, meaning that all who desired to follow his teaching were eligible.

Third Ecumenical Council 431 at Ephesus: Mary was given the title of Theotokes, Mother of God or God-bearer, at the Ecumenical Council. Another story regarding Mary's final days and death. According to this tradition, after Jesus' crucifixion, the Virgin Mary was escorted by the disciple John to Ephesus, where she died. (Odyssey Magazine-March '01 Ephesus)

Urantia: Part IV Life and Teachings of Jesus. A transmitted day to day chronicle of Jesus' life.

Vestments of the Twelve Golden Bells on the Blue Robe: A golden bell and a pomegranate, on the hem of the robe round about. And it shall be upon Aaron when he ministers, and its sound shall be heard when he enters the holy place before the Lord and when he comes out, that he may not die. And you shall make a crown of pure gold, and engrave upon it, like the engravings of a signet, HOLINESS TO THE LORD. (G.36)

The bells were to warn God of the coming of the priest so that He could be ready and not be caught unexpectedly. (G.37)

Wedding Garment: from Christian Mysteries; represents the outer clothing of the mind. The "Wedding garment" (G,38) is symbolical of a state of consciousness in which there is special preparation for the union unique; in other words, our external thinking must be in harmony with the inner revelation before we can make complete union with the Christ.

The higher life essences accumulated in former life experiences are drawn about the head of the newborn child and form a halo as recognized in artists drawings of the Holy Family and the Saints. "Through love and service to human kind these ethers gradually form the "wedding garment" which encircles the entire body. The greater the accumulated soul powers from the past, the sooner this garment of the soul is fashioned in the present life."

First mentioned as being worn by Anna, Mary's mother when she went to meet Joachim at the Golden Gate. It signified the level of spiritual attainment of the Initiate.

The Golden Wedding Garment:The Spiritualized forces of the etheric sheath, the purified desire body, and the spiritualized mind, creates their radiant body light. This is the "golden wedding garment" which each disciple must be clothed before he can enter into the presence of the Christ. The golden vase of perfume which Mary sister of Lazarus bathed the Master's feet has a like meaning. (G.39)

Xavier: Writer of Persian History of Christ, though some what discounted by modern research contains a number of interesting insights including descriptions of mother Mary (G.40)

Zalome: Before Mary and Joseph reached Bethlehem, the child was born. Zalome was the first midwife who came to serve the Mother Mary. When Joseph asked the woman on the roof if she knew of a midwife she answered: "You are Joseph the husband of Mary," She came down and put on her finest apparel. When they entered the cave, they saw the child at his mother's breast. Zalome fell down and worshipped him. She was the first to recognize the Christ. (G.41)

End Notes

Authors note: This book is designed for the average reader who is dissatisfied with the limited information given about the Mother Mary in the traditional texts. The idea is to honor her for who she was and acknowledge her role in bringing the Great One, the Master Jesus into incarnation on this planet.

This view is provided by many years of researching the ancient texts some of which had been translated and retranslated. Others were merely stories to legitimize the Messiah from stories prophesied in the Old Testament..

Many of the references are obscure, out of print or from hard to find manuscripts. The author not being a linguist herself has had to rely on translations into English.

The Bibliography gives the source of the stories. Further study is up to the seeker.

Bibliography

(1) Anonymous.*The Lost Books of the Bible.* Ameridian Book.New American Library. 1926

(2) Elliot, J.K *The Apocryphal New Testament* Clarendon Press-Oxford 1926

(3) Fillmore, Charles, *Unity, Metaphysical Bible Dictionary.* Unity School of Christianity,1931

(4) Heline, Corinne, *The Blessed Virgin.* The New Age Press.1971Jerome, *Latin Vulgate:*

(5) Heline, Corinne *New Age Bible Interpretations*-New Age Press, 1961 *New Testament* vo. IV *Mystery of the Christos* vol. VII

(6) Hock, Ronald F. *The Scholars Bible* The Gospels of Thomas and James Polebridge Press, Santa Rosa, CA 1995

(7) Lewis, Spencer H. *The Mystical Life of Jesus* Rosicrucian Library vol VIII, Supreme Grand Lodge of Amorc, San Jose, CA 1929

(8) Miller, Robert J.ed. *The Complete Gospels.* Polbridge Press, 1994

(9) Montague,James Rhodes *Apocryphal New Testament-* Oxford at the Clarendon Press 1924
The Book of James, or Protevangelium,
Gospel of Thomas
Gospel of Pseudo-Matthew
Pistas Sophia
The Gospel of the Birth of Mary
The Arabic Gospel of the Infancy
The Armenian Gospel of the Infancy
The History of Joseph the Carpenter,
Death of Joseph
Coptic Lives of the Virgin
Syriac Narratives
(10) Pfeiffer, Charles F.& Harrison, Everett. F *The Wycliffe Bible Commentary,* The Southwestern Company,1962
(11) Urantia, *The Urantia Book,* Urantia Foundation,1955
(12) Latin Narrative or Pseudo-Melito
(13) Funk and Wagnalls, *New Standard Bible Dictionary. Garden City Books* 1936

Bibles

(15) Barker,Kenneth.ed *NIV Study Bible.* ZondervanPublishing House   1995
(16) King James version of the Holy Bible
(17) Lamsa, George M. *The Holy Bible.*A.J. Holman Company. 1957
(18) *New Catholic Edition of the Holy Bible.* Catholic Book Company 1957

Magazines-Articles

(19) Bible Review:Magazine
The Christian Apocryphal Preserved in
Art June 1997
The Annunciation- August 1998
Witnessing the Divine 12/01
The Favored One 12/01
Jesus Family 4/20
All in the Family 7/20
Magi In Art 12/01
Where Was Jesus Born 2/02
O Little Town of Nazareth 2/02
Odyssey: Magazine 3/01 Ephesus

The Masters of Art Depict the Holy Story

*The Story of Art: The Lives and Times of the
Great Masters*, Regina Shoolman and Charles
Slatkin Halcyon House New York by Blue
Ribbon Books14 West 49th Street,
New York, NY 1940

Cover: Murillo, The Immaculate Conception
Murillo, Immaculate Conception 1617-82
David, Gerald: Adoration of the Kings
Rafael: Sistine Madonna
Titian: Assumption of the Virgin

Plates taken from Bible Review Magazine
1997,2000 &2001

268

(600 CE) by Giotto: Anna and Joachim
Meeting at the Golden Gate.SCALA/Resource NY
Rodger Van Der Weyden: The Annunciation
The Metropolitian Musesum of Art
(1425) by Robert Campin, The Nativity,
Salome questions Mary's virginity.
SCALA/Resource NY
(1485) by Domenico Ghirlandaio, The
Adoration of the Shepherds. SCALA/Resource NY

Index

Index

Index

Index